# The Art of Becoming Human

# The Art of Becoming Human

## Patterns of Growth,
## The Adventure of Living,
## Love & Separation, Limitless Possibilities

*Mary E. Mercer, M.D.*

Prometheus Books

59 John Glenn Drive
Amherst, New York 14228-2197

Published 2002 by Prometheus Books

06 05 04 03 02    5 4 3 2 1

Library of Congress Cataloging-in-Publication Data

Mercer, Mary E.
        The art of becoming human : patterns of growth, the adventure of living, love & separation, limitless possibilities / Mary E. Mercer.
                p.    cm.
        Originally published: 1997.
        Includes bibliographical references.
        ISBN 1–57392–940–9 (pbk. : alk. paper)
        1. Self-actualization (Psychology) 2. Maturation (Psychology) I. Title.
BF637.S4 M46 2001
155.2'5—dc21                                                        2001048277

For my first family,

Clarence Hopkins Mercer, M.D.
Ella May Davison Mercer
Frank Alfred Mercer

and

for all my subsequent extended families

# Contents

7

# Preface to the Paperback Edition

When *The Art of Becoming Human* was first published, to my amazement, many readers confided that they immediately turned to the chapter concerning their own age, as if the book were a horoscope. They were more interested in the circumstances of their present life than in the cumulative effects of the past, ignoring the fact that every experience leaves its fingerprints upon the psyche and casts its assimilated shadow over future activities.

The intention of this book is not only to trace the stages we go through—from birth to old age—that make us who we are, but also to help us appreciate how our individual past history colors the "why" we have become as we are. In fact, for those readers interested in their horoscope, the first chapter on early childhood provides ample clues for understanding some of their specific personality traits. An unattractive characteristic, begun in childhood and never corrected by indulgent parents, can persist into adult life as an impediment to mature social behavior. Happier traits are always invaluable personality assets in both our private and public lives. All "personality cards" are already on the table between the ages of one and five, ready to be picked up and played.

The original working title of this book was *Love and Separation*, the theme that pervades all of human life. The roots of self-confidence lie deeply buried in the quality of our first exposure to the love and devotion of our parents. In time, the ability to separate from the safety and protection of their touch and presence in order to satisfy a budding curiosity about some enticing, out-of-reach novelty in the world beyond demands considerable self-confidence. A mother's willingness to let us venture forth helps the process of separation enormously, and our first attempts are a heady introduction to individual freedom.

The original title of the book was ultimately changed because it could be misunderstood as concerning love, separation, and divorce. However, the underlying reality that life consists of a succession of loves and separations remains no less true.

Plato tells us that Socrates' fundamental question about human existence was: In what way shall we live our life? All the quotations in the present book address this question in different ways, but with memorable clarity and eloquence. Baruch de Spinoza, for one, spoke of the supreme happiness of the truth beyond fame, fortune, and sex. The great writers of every time and place have addressed this same concern of how to live life. On her deathbed Gertrude Stein was reportedly asked, "What is the answer?" Her reply: "What is the question?"

Is the quest the all of it? We do not have to be philosophers to wonder about the meaning of our life. There are no neat categories of how to live, no prepackaged instructions, no learned methods. Our best guide lies in moments of intuition in which we feel a flash of infinitely valuable insight that we can trust.

Experience is all; no one can teach us. Truth comes in unexpected flashes that cannot be captured or recalled at will, but the memory of its essence, its unique and mysterious reality, remains indelible, a permanent possession, our talisman. This truth quiets the busyness of our minds and leaves us silent and unafraid, extremely conscious of what is most dear to us. It becomes a trusted guide in showing us harmonious ways to live our own particular life by profoundly influencing our actions and activities.

One of the most confirming insights we can attain is that the repetition of love and separation offers us a second chance. If our family life in early childhood has been happy, we know how to repeat it in our future adult family life; if our childhood family life has been unfortunate, we have a second chance to create a happier family life for our own children and for ourselves as parents. It is within our power to do something about the quality of our adult years.

Finally, the privilege of reaching old age, which is increasingly attainable, offers us a second chance to live quietly, with our past public and private activities at peace with each other, to remember what cannot be taught, to accept the results of our inevitable encounters of love and separation with grace and compassion, and to love life no matter how it is.

The key word in the title *The Art of Becoming Human* is, of course, "becoming." To be human in its best sense is to treat others as we wish to be treated. It takes time to learn how to *become* human.

This book will stir up painful memories of moments in each of our lives when we have failed at being human in our behavior toward others. Separation resulted. Only the pain of recognition of our inhumanity will help us to seek forgiveness.

The purpose of a long life is to recover from the dark, secret love of our own opinions, and to acknowledge the blaze of truth in every moment, which helps us to become wiser and more understanding and compassionate with each other.

# *Preface*

The impetus to write this book came from observations gathered over a period of more than fifty years in the practice of child and adult psychiatry. My training and experience in internal medicine, pediatrics, and psychiatry provided the opportunity and privilege of witnessing the unfolding of every stage in human life.

Rather than use for illustration personal anecdotes from my or my patients' lives, I have chosen powerful examples from great literature to reveal the universal pattern that lies deeply buried beneath the economic, social, and political surface of individual life. We need to be reminded that long before the formulation of psychiatric concepts about human behavior there existed the penetrating, lyrical, enlightening commentaries of poets and writers.

The intention of this book is to bring together these two modes of expression—the scientific and the artistic—and to trace the continuum that carries the infant into late adulthood, that allows the experience of a person living four centuries ago to be pertinent to us today in the third millennium, that makes the voice of Shakespeare or James Joyce continue to resonate with words that impregnate our spirit and show us a mirror image of ourselves.

My personal perspective owes much to specific individuals: my parents, who introduced me to the harmony within a congenial family; the teachers who laid out before me the realms of literature and medicine; the children in pediatrics who taught me how to see; the adult patients who taught me how to listen; and the friends of a lifetime who taught me how to love without qualification. Among these, I would specifically like to mention Adele Morrison; Marianne Kris, M.D.; M. R. Jarno; Steven Mitchell; and Elizabeth Trupin, all of whom helped me to bring this book to fruition.

*Run to me with your feet,*
*race to me with your legs;*
*For I have a word to tell you,*
*a story to recount to you:*
*The word of the tree and the charm*
*of the stone,*
*The whisper of the heavens to the earth,*
*of the seas to the stars.*

From the Epic of Baal (Canaanite)

Mary E. Mercer, M.D.
Nyack, New York

# Introduction

*T*o become a human being is not easy. The fact that we are born and grow physically without our conscious participation does not mean that becoming a human being is an inevitable, automatic process. We have to do something about it. We participate in the process and have the potential to affect many aspects of it. How we live our lives, how we think, how we react to our experiences, how we would wish to be—rather than how we are—all contribute to our humanness or lack of it.

This book considers not only the common experiences of human growth from birth to old age, but the profound influence that endowment, chance, necessity, and hope play in individual lives. Into this inquiry I have also found it useful to weave reflections and comments left for our edification, comfort, and pleasure by some of the world's most knowledgeable observers of the human condition.

Feeling colors our experiences at each step of development. Our first love in earliest childhood is for things—milk and honey, and blanket warmth. Our second love is for people. We begin to love those people who feed and comfort us, until, gradually, they become more important to us than the things they provide.

This pattern of love for comforting things first and comforting people second repeats itself endlessly, until one day, if we are extraordinarily fortunate, our desire to be loved is transformed into a desire to love. We may become sharply aware that the state of being a lover is more enviable than the state of being a beloved. It is the lover who is enabled to take the first step toward becoming a human being with all of its sudden joy and goodness, as well as anguish.

Falling in love is not, of course, to be mistaken for loving. All too often we fail wretchedly when we fall in love. And almost certainly before we are able to love, privation and suffering have become our teachers. To love means to overcome our fear, sorrow, and hurt, so that we are free to see another person with sympathy, and to understand and welcome the life that surrounds us, whatever it is. The significant change occurs when our compassion overwhelms our passion.

How is this transformation to be accomplished? What is this force that penetrates our self-absorption and sets our hearts on fire? Happenstance has been said to be the result of poor planning, but the happenings along the way that help us to become human have nothing to do with planning. Once we are drawn beyond our ordinary egocentric limits by the power that comes of loving something superior to ourselves, nothing is ever the same. Suddenly, we are on a quest for something that is forever ours, something that sets us free to live without conflict or fear, something that, in Spinoza's words, cannot be lost, cannot be taken away, and cannot be diminished by another person loving it, too.

There is no special time or place for such an experience; it can happen at any moment of our lives. But the sooner it occurs, the more fortunate the person.

There are marvelously informed guides, familiar with this way of living, who, having gone before us, have left behind their words to help us, to encourage us, and to strengthen us. Henry David Thoreau knew all about this adventure when he wrote in *Walden,*

> I long ago lost a hound dog, a bay horse, and a turtle dove, and am still on their trail. Many are the travellers I have spoken to concerning them, describing their tracks and what calls they answered to. I have met one or two who have heard the hound, the tramp of the horse, and even seen the dove disappear behind a cloud, and they seemed as anxious to recover them as if they had lost them themselves.

When Joseph Campbell was asked how to embark upon such a quest, he said, "Follow your bliss." In a longer statement in his book *The Hero with a Thousand Faces,* he wrote,

> We have only to follow the thread of the hero path. And where we have thought to find an abomination, we shall find a god; and where we have thought to travel outward, we shall come to the center of our existence; when we had thought to be alone, we shall be with all the world.

To be struck by an outer living force that penetrates to the core of our being, that rescues us from error in the midst of a self-centered, misguided existence, that obliges us to begin a new, untried, exacting search—of our own making, for our own meaning—is to be longed for, hoped for, and pursued.

This book is not a blueprint to happiness, nor is it strictly a "how-to" guide to humanness. Rather, it seeks to lay out the choices that can lead us all from passion to compassion, which is the highest possible state of understanding and freedom that a human being can attain.

# 1

# *Early Childhood (Birth to Five Years)*

*T*he adventure of becoming a human being begins with separation from the mother's womb, the first of many separations. Throughout life, separation from the known to the unknown invariably precedes each new, successive stage of human growth.

> Even as the sun and planets stood to salute one another on the day we entered the world—even so, we began straightaway to grow and have continued to do so according to the law that prevailed over our beginning. It is thus that we must be, we cannot escape ourselves . . . no time nor power can destroy the shape that has been impressed upon our evolving life.
>
> Johann Wolfgang von Goethe
> "First, Last Words, Orphic: Destiny"

A newborn baby is so different from the rest of us that most adults are content to smile at him and leave him with his mother, which is exactly what he wants himself.

# The Art of Becoming Human

His human potential lies totally undeveloped but ready to be aroused by contact with his mother. What happens between them defies easy comprehension, thanks to its complexity and its intensity. Whether boy or girl, the same awakening occurs between a newborn and the mother.*

A newborn knows nothing about his father but he has experienced his mother in a unique and intimate way—with a deep, blind knowledge of her body. Even though he does not know how she looks, he knows how she sounds.

Inside her womb the rhythm of her heartbeat has drummed into his subconsciousness; her breathing has been close to his ears; her voice has vibrated through the amniotic fluid; her walk has rocked him to sleep; any pressure on her abdominal wall was transmitted to him through the uterine wall. He has heard the gurgle of her stomach and intestines and the sound of her bowels. And the tension of her feelings has stirred them both. In turn his mother has been aware of him from the day she first felt him kick. A secret communication springs up between them, known consciously only by her.

After the shock of birth, physical contact with the mother's body comforts the newborn as nothing else can. The rhythm of her heartbeat and breathing are familiar links between the lost paradise of uterine existence and this strange, new, earthly reality.

The newborn's expulsion from the crushing compression of the birth canal is only the prelude to further ordeals. To help his breathing he may be slapped; to drain mucous from his respiratory tract he may be hung by his heels. He has used his head as a battering ram to push his way through the birth canal; surely, it aches. There is much to cry about at birth.

The change in his environment could not be more drastic. For nine months he has lived in the warm, dark, quiet waters of his

---

*The use of an editorial "he" will refer to both sexes.

mother's womb with its muffled sounds and swaying motion, supported by soft, floating membranes. Suddenly—after terrifying, rhythmic compression—he is thrust into the environment of the delivery room where his unorganized, unintegrated senses are explosively assaulted by glaring lights, loud voices, and moving people. The abrupt immersion into air with its antiseptic odor irritates his nose, mouth, and throat. The rigidity of a steel scale makes his back arch in protest; the stiffness of cloth is a far cry from the softness of the womb. After the loss of a safe, small, confining space, how is he ever to find rest and satisfaction again?

When he is placed over his mother's heart, he discovers his first reassuring sign of continuity—he hears and feels the familiar heartbeat. He relaxes slightly into her breathing. The once-muffled sound of her voice and laughter is now clear and distinct. Buried far down in his subconsciousness, these subtle, identifying impressions of the mother—unthought by him and unknown to his mother—remain with the newborn forever.

Different cultures have different ceremonies to celebrate the uniqueness of the newborn. In Bali, for instance, a newborn is treated as a gift of God until his 105th day. Then he is brought to the temple priest, who welcomes him to life on earth by placing his feet upon the ground for the first time.

Many people in Western civilization find the uniqueness of the newborn, as celebrated by Wordsworth's poem, especially appealing.

> Our birth is but a sleep and a forgetting:
> The Soul that rises with us, our life's Star,
> Hath had elsewhere its setting,
> And cometh from afar:
> Not in entire forgetfulness,
> And not in utter nakedness,

# The Art of Becoming Human

But trailing clouds of glory do we come
From God, who is our home:
Heaven lies about us in our infancy.

William Wordsworth
"Ode: Intimations of Immortality
from Recollections of Early Childhood"

A newborn's quality of otherness is well known—even his mother is aware that her baby is an intimate stranger. In the first weeks of life the infant spends the entire twenty-four hours sleeping or nursing, oblivious to the external world. His parents, having dreamt about him for nine months, delight in looking at him, touching him, talking to him. Gradually he begins to stay awake for ever-longer periods of time and tries to focus his eyes.

At his mother's breast he explores with his sucking mouth; and with waving arms and thrusting legs, he touches her. He hears, smells, tastes, and touches before he sees her clearly.

His first attention is centered upon her face. He gazes at her impersonally from a great distance—a sovereign distance—as if she were a fascinating, strange object. It is a gaze without recognition. She, eager for recognition, banishes that objective, impersonal gaze by covering the baby's face with kisses. He is helpless; kisses are nice, but his inscrutable, unfathomable separateness—his integrity—remains intact.

This unalterable quality of otherness, a fixed, permanent gulf separating human beings from one another, is inviolable. It is the precious isolation of the self, which, as Rilke has said, can only be bordered on, protected, and saluted.

How shall I guard my soul so that it be
Not touched by thine? And how shall it be brought,
Lifted above thee, unto other things?

Ah, gladly would I hide it utterly
Lost in the dark where are no murmurings,
In strange and silent places that do not
Vibrate when thy deep soul quivers and sings.
But all that touches us two makes us twin,
Even as the bow crossing the violin
Draws but one voice from the two strings that meet.
Upon what instrument are we two spanned?
And what great player has us in his hand?
O sweet song.

Rainer Maria Rilke
"The Song of Love"

Intimate as mother and baby are, a nursing couple, they always will remain separate, unique individuals, different not only from each other but from everyone else in the world.

A baby's love for his mother starts with her, not him. She is the lover, he the beloved. Let it be said, his first love is stomach love; he loves food long before he loves the one who feeds him. Nothing satisfies him, at first, but food. His whole waking life centers around feeding and he never allows his parents to forget it. The look of unadulterated bliss on the face of a satiated infant is unmistakable. Once his stomach is full, he loses interest and falls asleep.

The father and mother love their newborn—who is in need of absolutely everything—asking nothing in return. Most frequently they feel useful, not used, as they learn the meaning of his body language. By keeping him comfortable—warm, clean, dry, fed—the mother courts the baby into a relationship of trust with her. Baby care is not difficult, but it is endless and can be exhausting. Only love makes it possible for young parents to lose sleep, to sacrifice their own pleasures, perhaps for the first time over such a protracted period, for the sake of the baby.

# The Art of Becoming Human

Parents grow and develop, too. Day and night they must get up to take care of the baby whether they want to or not. They have to win the willingness of their own hearts to use their energies for the infant's benefit, to share the workload with each other, to pull together, to be aware of each other's stamina. The presence of the baby may help them to mature faster than almost anything else. Little did they realize that one particular night of love secretly contained the simple force, the further impulse, the unforeseen furtherance of their own development as human beings.

> We are told nothing of conception, really nothing at all.
> Only the firelit symbols of an antique nurse scary and
>     changing on the wall.
> We are told nothing
> Of the vibrato of desire remorseless
> Until the solar-plexal swinging
> Orchestrates to all flesh singing.
> Post coitum, omnia tristia sunt.
> Sadness, then sleep, the blaze of noon, love's gladness.
>
> There was no witness of this bridal night
> Only azoic seascape and interlocking angels' might.
> So now we speculate with filial wonder
> Fabricate that night of love, and ponder
> On the quietude of Satan in our Father's arms:
> Velocity stilled, the restful shade.
> Satan we can understand—but what was God's will
> That cosmic night before we were made?

Carson McCullers
"Hymen, O Hymen"*

---

After weeks of daily routines, one day the mother suddenly realizes that the baby is quietly studying her. The scrutiny will continue until her identity is firmly established as the source of his comfort. It is a recognition for all time, profoundly gratifying to the mother. She becomes the infant's external world.

The father may feel somewhat sidelined at times, especially if the baby is breast fed. He cannot be a substitute mother, even though he may share the chores of baby care. By supporting his wife emotionally during this first year, he makes an inestimable contribution to the welfare of his offspring. In due time he will forge his own indelible bond with the baby.

Mothering is synonymous with protecting. The mother identifies with her baby—when he hurts, she hurts. Indeed, in the quality of her care is buried the secret message of his bodily worth, the seed of his future self-regard.

In time he imitates his mother's facial expressions. She is not necessarily aware that she is a model of behavior, but inadvertently she teaches him her likes and dislikes, a castor oil grimace, for instance.

At six months the mother can no longer hand the baby over to a stranger without his indignant protest. The earlier, smiling, unprejudiced days are over. Now he clings to his mother with all his might; he wants no part of anyone he does not know. He is a person to be reckoned with, a person who wants only his mother.

By eight months he is even more demanding and dependent. He does not want his mother out of sight. If she puts him in a playpen and leaves the room, he cries as if abandoned forever. The sound of her voice is not enough—what he wants is to *see* her.

An infant is first a touching, tasting, smelling person—a contact person. Then he becomes a seeing person. At first he feels his mother is a physical part of himself, but gradually he sees that she is separate, with the ability to come and go. Sight introduces him to space, which he can endure more easily if his mother stays within view.

When she is out of sight, hearing becomes his new tool in coping with space. If she disappears into the next room, he hears her, which is better than silence only because it helps him to believe in the possibility of her return.

For him to shift from one sensory orientation to another in connection with objects in space is a remarkably complicated process, as well as the first liberating impulse in trying to stem the despair of separation.

The physical achievements in the first year of an infant's life are truly extraordinary. At first a helpless newborn in a prone position, he not only rises to his feet, however unsteadily, but sits, grasps, and crawls by himself. With help he walks. He even says a few words, and has a few teeth. Only 365 days separate his newborn liquid diet of warm, sweet milk from his one-year-old's high-chair plate of chopped meat and vegetables, a cup of milk, and pudding. Never again will he develop so many skills so quickly.

His mother, who has been his partner all the way, now begins to reap the fruits of their symbiosis. He treats her as if he owns her! Increasingly, she wishes to escape, for she has trouble finding time for herself or anyone else apart from him.

In the latter half of the first year, emotionally dependent and highly possessive, a baby loves his mother with all the tyranny of infantile passion. In his glory he becomes opinioned, and high-chair arguments signal the beginning of the struggle between individual wills. Who knows best? The mother has her reasons and feelings; he has only his feelings. He has learned to trust his mother, but he has yet to learn that she is something other than his utter servant, or that she can differ with him and still love him.

He does not know that the waning of their symbiotic days heralds a gradual loosening of their coupling with an inevitable dilution of their intimacy—the next step in his development. There always remains, however, a special mutuality between them that may contain, for him, a sprouting initiative and growing independence without loss of love, and for his mother, a longed-for freedom from the oppressive at-oneness with him.

Exasperated mothers call the daily confrontation that characterizes the next stage of development "the terrible twos." The sweet commingling of infancy is steadily eroded by the sharp cleavage of individual desires and intentions.

Increasingly, the baby is a me-do-it person. He insists upon trying to feed himself, the result of which is an unbelievable mess. He uses his fingers. He plays with food, spits it out, throws it around, empties it on his high-chair tray, his head, his mother. He is not being deliberately naughty nor is he trying to be funny. He is simply impulsive and experimental.

He and his mother may have different ideas of what he will eat and how much he will eat. His feelings outrank her wishes, for only he knows what tastes good and when he is satisfied.

The time and effort necessary to prepare a meal—which he may refuse to eat—is not within his range of understanding. The question is: whose food is it? If the mother considers it hers—because she prepared it—and he rejects it, she feels rejected. If she considers the food his—once it is on his plate—then his pleasure or disdain measures his hunger rather than her effort.

Eating is a simple, direct, enjoyable, personal experience unless robbed of its innocence by highly charged emotional contaminants. For a toddler to be asked to eat for his mother's sake, not solely for his own, is deeply troublesome. What happens, then, if he is angry with her? To refuse to eat is a very poor way to express anger, especially if its cause has no connection with food.

During this second year a child is called a toddler because his balance is so precarious that he has to walk with a wide base. To learn to walk requires remarkable persistence and patience; he pulls himself erect and tentatively steps forward and falls, then tries again and falls again, over and over. When he finally solves the problem of balance, his joy is contagious, a wonder to anyone fortunate enough to behold it.

As soon as he can manage a few consecutive steps, he toddles straight to his mother. If she disappears into the next room, he follows her. He has discovered that the power of locomotion gives him the ability to end unwanted separation, as well as a new freedom of action in all directions.

Very often he pays for this new mobility with physical pain, from which his mother tries to protect him. She sees dangers that he does not. Her warning cries alert him to incalculable possibilities of catastrophe. He touches the stove, he climbs onto tables, he slams a door on his fingers, he knocks over heavy objects onto his toes. He breaks bones and swallows foreign objects. He reaches for the handle of a simmering pan. It takes a lively imagination to anticipate the range of incessant activity that surprises his mother afresh each day.

The toddler also breaks things. A canny mother puts her most cherished possessions out of reach—safer yet, out of sight—thus avoiding direct conflict between her love for her child and her love for her possessions. The breakage is not deliberate; he is not mean, just clumsy. His insatiable curiosity tempts him to touch everything within sight, even though he has no idea of the value of anything. Curiosity, the taproot of all learning, lures him daily into exploration.

As the horizon of the toddler's world enlarges, he pays more and more attention to his siblings, if he has any, and their possessions. When he tries to join their play he is too disruptive to be welcome, but because he is so blissfully self-centered, he barely notices his rejection, particularly if he has succeeded in taking possession of one of their coveted toys. He is not unlike the mythological dragon that hoards gold and young maidens even though it has no idea of what to do with them.

Animals by no means escape his attention, and he can be relied upon to treat them roughly. The look in the eyes of the family dog is mute witness to previous unhappy experiences. When the toddler heads in his direction, he tries to slink away unnoticed. The family cat, of course, has already disappeared.

Space once again becomes a terrible problem at bedtime, when it occurs to the toddler that if he goes to sleep, how can he be sure that his mother is still there? Sleep does separate them temporarily, but he fears that the separation might be permanent.

The mother's soothing, promising words fall on deaf ears. Words are less persuasive than actions; her presence, here and now, is more concrete than her promised return in the morning. The father, a long-familiar figure, likewise fails to comfort. Trust, an abstract idea, is rigorously tested each night by the toddler's insufferable demands. He needs another particular toy for company, he wants a glass of water, he has a question, he wants another kiss, he has a complaint—anything to keep them with him, until, finally, he succumbs to sleep.

Slowly, reluctantly, the toddler begins to accept the mother's promises in place of her presence. Even though he does not greet babysitters with joy, when the mother leaves him during the day or when both parents go out at night, he will gradually, with very poor grace, permit his parents to depart.

# The Art of Becoming Human

My sole consolation when I went upstairs for the night was that Mamma would come in and kiss me after I was in bed. But this goodnight lasted for so short a time: she went down again so soon that the moment in which I heard her climb the stairs, and then caught the sound of her garden dress of blue muslin . . . rustling along the double-doored corridor, was for me a moment of the keenest sorrow. So much did I love that good-night that I reached the stage of hoping that it would come as late as possible, so as to prolong the time of respite during which Mamma would not yet have appeared. Sometimes when, after kissing me, she opened the door to go, I longed to call her back, to say to her "Kiss me just once more again," but I knew that then she would at once look displeased, for the concession which she made to my wretchedness and agitation in coming up to me with this kiss of peace always annoyed my father, who thought such ceremonies absurd, and she would have liked to try to induce me to outgrow the need, the custom of having her there at all, which was a very different thing from letting the custom grow up of my asking her for an additional kiss when she was already crossing the threshold. And to see her look displeased destroyed all the sense of tranquility she had brought me a moment before, when she bent her loving face down over my bed, and held it out to me like a Host, for an act of Communion in which my lips might drink deeply the sense of her real presence, and with it the power to sleep. But those evenings on which Mamma stayed so short a time in my room were sweet indeed compared to those on which we had guests to dinner, and therefore she did not come at all.

Marcel Proust
*Swann's Way*

A toddler's love for his mother is double-edged, making every detrimental claim of exclusive love on the one hand, while

30

on the other awakening in him a desire to please, to make sacrifices for her. Love makes a giver out of him for the first time. Giving never happens in a vacuum; it has to be activated. For a toddler to do the things that delight his mother but are of immense nuisance to himself takes great love.

Possibly the ultimate sacrifice that the toddler makes for his mother is toilet training. She decides to introduce him to the bathroom facilities and suggests that it would be very nice if he used them.

Nice for whom? Why should he endure the discomfort of a full bladder or a distended bowel when a diaper so easily takes care of the problem?

Does his mother appreciate how hard it is to calculate the time and distance between where he happens to be and the bathroom? Occasionally he tells her of his need, but usually not in time. It demands his utmost concentration to achieve a successful meshing of all these logistics. And when he finally succeeds, he is in for a great shock.

His bowels, the center of so much attention from his mother, have taken on a reflected importance for him. He treats feces as he treats every other interesting object: he wants to touch, to taste, to smell. Unlike his mother, he has no prejudice. In one stroke, she is delighted with his act and repelled by the product. He has to learn to hate the result of his efforts, which is beyond understanding.

At this point he is likely to make a surprising discovery concerning power and revenge. He finds out that his bowels are his and their product is his to give or to withhold. No one can make him empty his bowels and *that* is power. When he wishes to please, he gives; when he is angry, he withholds. He utilizes his bowel and bladder to express his feelings—particularly about his mother.

These choices lift him to another level of self-regard. The power to give pleasure or displeasure, the power to consent or to refuse distinguishes him in his own eyes. It offers him an unexpected status apart from his mother that slightly shifts the balance between them. He becomes more his own person. The feel of his autonomy is good; his riveted attention upon his mother begins to wane ever so slightly.

Independence from his mother has its beginning when he starts to leave her, not when she leaves him. It signals a significant separation. At first, curiosity lures him away. When absolutely sure of her presence, he begins to look around. Everything he sees invites him to come closer for a better look.

From a bench beside a sandbox in any public park, it is possible to see the reeling-out and the reeling-in of an invisible cord attaching a toddler to his mother. The invisible cord is like a psychic leash. The mother sits still. He presses against her knee while watching the sandbox activity. Intrigued, he takes a few experimental steps toward the sandbox and away from his mother. Suddenly, he brings himself up short. Is she still there? He turns to look. She smiles. Reassured, the invisible leash reels out a little more. He toddles a few more steps away.

How long it takes the toddler to feel comfortable with his new independence will differ from child to child. It is a complicated process involving his initiative, the mother's willingness to let him go, and his trust that she will not leave him when his back is turned. It truly is a joint venture based on nonverbal trust, understanding, and reciprocity.

A toddler meets other toddlers as one potentate meets another. Knowing nothing about sharing, fair play, consideration, or civility, they treat each other as interesting objects, as toys. Their callous capriciousness needs the presence of a judicious adult to keep their brief, dramatic encounters peaceful. The mother acts as a bridge from the private world of family, where he is her little darling, to the public world of strangers, where he is one among many.

The mother's immediate intervention is needed to settle the vehement disputes that inevitably follow in the toddler's wake. There is a tenacious ruthlessness about his desires that makes him try to take what he wants, if he can. Rightful ownership means nothing to him; in truth, he is a marauding barbarian who badly needs to be civilized.

It is natural to have desires, but a very young child does not know that there may be a price to be paid in fulfilling them. He wants everything free, on demand. It is his mother's civilizing voice that introduces him to the alien concept of the rights of others.

If he does not learn now to consider his neighbor as himself, he will continue to consider himself first, last, and always. This unfortunate characteristic will continue to operate long after he is old enough to have outgrown it, bringing incalculable distress to others and preserving in him a highly unattractive personality trait.

When he occasionally puts aside his lust for playthings in order to join other children as a welcomed member of a play group, he experiences a new type of gratification—companion-ship—that makes him giddy with pleasure. When playing with a playmate becomes more agreeable than playing alone with a toy, what he gains humanly is more than what he loses materially.

As yet the toddler does not understand time, that is, clock time, but he knows the time of his routines. Promises made according to routine-time begin to be understood. His language is developing, too, as understanding leaps beyond the tone of voice to the meaning of a word. His babbling attempts to follow the shape of words, and then to form the pattern of a sentence. This new dimension of communication pleases him enormously and is reinforced by lavish praise from everyone, especially his parents.

To his astonishment and chagrin, the toddler gradually becomes aware that other people make claims upon *his* mother, and that she acts as if they have every right to do so. It becomes more and more plain that he is not her only beloved, and as he watches her act tenderly toward a sibling, he senses a situation without a solution. From then on the toddler is plunged into the society of his family, a society of rivals for his mother's attention. It is a state about which he can do little but bitterly accept, for it is better to have his share of her love than to be without it entirely.

Once his high-handed treatment of his mother as his exclusive possession is tempered, love makes the toddler a supplicant. His mother uses this change of attitude to teach him more socially acceptable behavior: he learns manners, especially table manners. He really does not want to be bothered about the details of polite behavior, nor does he have the slightest understanding of the reason for her requests, but her approval or disapproval counts, so he tries to cooperate to please her.

The birth of a new sibling, however, is his mother's worst betrayal. When he realizes that the newborn is not an interesting visitor, but is going to stay permanently, usurping his place as the youngest, he suffers genuine heartbreak. Why does she need this baby when she has him?

If he could speak his thoughts they might resemble those that Shakespeare put into the mind of Cleopatra, who seeks to learn the attributes of Octavia after hearing that Antony has married her.

> I faint. O Iras! Charmian! Tis no matter.
> Go to the fellow, good Alexas; bid him
> Report the feature of Octavia: her years,
> Her inclination, let him not leave out

The color of her hair. Bring me word quickly.
. . . [I] . . . Bid you Alexas.
Bring me word how tall she is. Pity me, Charmian
But do not speak to me. Lead me to my chamber.

William Shakespeare
*Antony and Cleopatra*
Act 2, scene 5

During this period of despair the child would dearly love to get rid of the new baby. Family photographs plainly show his distress and sadness. If he is forced to pretend that he loves this intruder, his hug will practically strangle the infant.

Since, unlike Shakespeare, he has no words to express his dismay, he acts out his thoughts and feelings by attempting a temporary retreat to infancy. He competes with the baby. He demands a bottle and a diaper. But it is too late. He cannot grow backward. Sadly he realizes that his new task consists of charming his mother with himself, just as he is, which is exactly, he finds out, what pleases her the most.

If he is the eldest child, he suffers probably the deepest wound from the birth of another sibling. For only the oldest can know what it was like to be an only child, and to have his mother's complete attention focused upon him alone.

If he is the youngest, he will suffer the least. He keeps the prerogatives of being the baby in the family and never knows the pangs of being supplanted.

If he is the middle child, he is a nonperson to his older sibling and demoted in status by the new baby.

If he is a member of a large family, he is not necessarily better off. Every birth reduces the share of attention each child can expect from his parents, particularly the mother. Various alliances—often defense pacts—spring up between pairs of siblings.

35

# The Art of Becoming Human

An only child is not challenged by competition at home with other children and does not have to fight to prove anything. If the outside world becomes too rough and disorderly, he can always retreat to the peaceful security of home. Among siblings there is no retreat, but there is company. Sibling jealousy can cast a long shadow. If it gets buried alive or pushed aside and never resolved, the hurt feelings can remain bruised and sore for a lifetime. Occasionally, after years of distance or disinterest, siblings may rediscover each other as adults. If there are good reasons for respect and admiration to develop between them, their rescued friendship can provide one of life's most rewarding experiences. This new relationship, saturated as it is with bittersweet nostalgia, is made up partly of remembrance of things past, partly of shared, haunting, almost unconscious, ancient familiarity.

In fact, the reclaiming of a lost sibling may awaken a sympathy for the entire family of man.

> Whoever weeps somewhere out in the world,
> Weeps without cause in the world,
> Weeps over me.
>
> Whoever laughs somewhere out in the night,
> Laughs without cause in the night,
> Laughs at me.
>
> Whoever wanders somewhere in the world,
> Wanders in vain in the world,
> Wanders towards me.
>
> Whoever dies somewhere in the world,
> Dies without cause in the world,
> Looks at me.

> Rainer Maria Rilke
> "Silent Hour"

Sibling jealousy does not exist among children who have no parents; under such circumstances siblings cling together. They need to belong to someone. They need to be expected somewhere, even if only by each other.

When the child is between three and five years, he is forced by circumstances to relinquish his autocratic ways, to share his possessions with siblings or playmates, and to become an acceptable family member. If he has older siblings, he, the smaller and weaker child, grudgingly grants their older claims, rights, and privileges. In turn, they stop treating him as a nonperson and begin to take him more seriously. He can no longer take their possessions with impunity; in fact, they may take his. But the pleasure of being included and of sharing in their activities, even on an unfair basis, is surprisingly sweet.

The camaraderie that develops apart from the mother is new, and it even changes her role somewhat. She is important but no longer exclusively stage center. In any quarrel she remains the final arbitrator, even though the supreme court of last appeal is usually the father.

Differences of opinion with the mother increase, but the child's physical attachment to her is still intimate, though less markedly so than during the infancy and toddler periods.

The mother's role shifts slightly, too, with the emergence of the child's abilities to climb, run, jump, dance, and skip, to open and shut, to hold on and let go, to empty and fill, to fit together and take apart. In developing these new skills, the favorite leader, by far, is the father, who now becomes the center of attention.

The preschool child delights in new enterprises with the father, so utterly and wonderfully different from the mother. With or without the birth of a sibling, he turns away from his mother, almost with relief, to give his devotion to his father.

# The Art of Becoming Human

Although his feelings for his father are complex and will become more so as time goes by, a three-year-old child returns his father's love openly, gladly, delightedly, without stint. In every possible way the father is loved, admired, and imitated.

Up to this age the use of the pronoun "he" has referred to a boy or a girl interchangeably because very little boys and girls develop along much the same lines, despite the difference in sex. But now, gender begins to make a demonstrable difference in their actions and reactions.

When a little girl turns to her father, she begins a relationship with a large future. Here is a man to admire, whose power is surely superior to her mother's. Her father's knowledge, his strength, his authority, the sight and smell of him, the deep voice and rougher touch, are a marvel and delight. Love for him floods her heart as she becomes unabashedly her daddy's girl. Who is the betrayer now?

And her father, responding to her charm, is utterly captivated.

> Frail the white rose and frail are
> Her hands that gave
> Whose soul is sere and paler
> Than time's wan wave.
>
> Rosefrail and fair—yet frailest
> A wonder wild
> In gentle eyes thou veilest,
> My blueveined child.
>
> James Joyce
> "A Flower Given to My Daughter"

The little boy, too, is particularly conscious of his father's size and strength. He, too, marvels at the many things that his father can do, and is thrilled by his willingness to show him how things work. He treats his father as a sage—able to answer all questions—and as a storyteller without equal. Trips with him, even a walk around the block, are a boundlessly exciting exploration. The boy loves the movements and mannerisms of his father, which he tries to imitate in every possible way with the most generous admiration.

The haunting scent of the outside world clings differently to the father than to a working mother and is part of his attraction. Ready to enter and enjoy this wider world, both girl and boy have better control of their large and small muscles, and better command of speech. They are also clean, dry, and more socially adaptable. These refinements equip them to proudly accompany their father out in public and to partake of all kinds of new experiences. Social acceptance by others puts them in high good humor, and their sunniness attracts an admiring audience almost everywhere they go. Everyone is charmed by the way they look and behave, but no one more so than they themselves.

Better physical coordination ensures fewer accidents. Preschool children now accept without protest certain known facts: fire burns, knives cut, needles prick, and a banister prevents a fall. Nevertheless, they still expect their mother to guard them from unknown hazards. With their father they sense that they are less closely watched and, accordingly, able to explore with greater freedom. Less protective than their mother, he is reluctant to curb their curiosity. As they become better able to use and retain what they learn, they find that these very qualities are especially appealing to their father.

# The Art of Becoming Human

My impression as a child always was that my father was not very much older than we were. He used to take us to sail our boats in the Round Pond, and with his own hands fitted one out with masts and sails after the patterns of a Cornish lugger; and we knew that his interest was no "grown up" pretense; it was as genuine as our own; so there was a perfectly equal companionship between us.

Virginia Woolf
"Impressions of Sir Leslie Stephen"


The curiosity of preschool children makes them the first spectators at any scene of excitement. Sirens of fire trucks, police cars, and ambulances are powerful magnets. Everything they see, they relate to themselves and view as good or bad, black or white, with no relieving grays.

It is not difficult to discover the thoughts of children: ask them and they tell you. They are without guile; their answers are usually astonishingly original, and often unabashedly grim. What they see and hear on sidewalks is kaleidoscopic, and everything they see competes indiscriminately for their attention.

They believe easily, therefore they are easily frightened. What is obvious to adults may be mysterious to them. Their grasp of what is real and what is imaginary is slippery at best, often leading to confusion about which is which. Fairy tales can be hair-raising to preschool children, and exposure to traumatic situations, in life or on television, may have far-reaching consequences. When their imagination peoples the dark with witches, ghosts, and burglars, when broken things are the source of fearful speculation, when punishment follows error, they dream bad dreams, wake in terror, and flee to the safety of their parents' bed for comfort until they are calm enough to go back to their own.

No one escapes these experiences, not even Goethe!

Unfortunately, too, the principle of discipline that young persons should be early deprived of all fear for the awful and invisible, and accustomed to the terrible, still prevailed. We children, therefore, were compelled to sleep alone, and when we found this impossible, and softly slipped from our beds to seek the society of the servants and maids, our father, with his dressing gown turned inside out, which disguised him sufficiently for the purpose, placed himself in the way, and frightened us back to our resting places. The evil effect of this anyone may imagine. How is he who is encompassed with a double terror to be emancipated from fear? My mother, always cheerful and gay, and willing to render others so, discovered a much better pedagogical expedient. She managed to gain her ends by rewards. It was the season for peaches, the plentiful enjoyment of which she promised us every morning if we overcame our fears during the night. In this way she succeeded, and both parties were satisfied.

Johann Wolfgang von Goethe
*Truth and Poetry*

Despite the irrational fears of children of this age, make-believe remains their favorite game and the source of much delight, *if* they can imitate what they already know. Sometimes it becomes the source of fright, if they cannot control the intrusiveness of a startling idea suggested by an adult trying to liven things up.

Left alone, the play of preschool children is of high seriousness while it lasts. They are totally committed to it and never seem to run out of ideas. They make free use of found objects, faithfully acting out what they have witnessed, usually at home. Being supremely unselfconscious of their uncensored acts, their transparency is endearing just as long as the secrets they make visible belong to somebody else.

41

# The Art of Becoming Human

Occasionally they embarrass their parents by what they say publicly. By age four they have found their tongues. Their questions are endlessly challenging and provocative. Where is nowhere? Where does daylight go when nighttime comes? What happens to people when they die? Where do babies come from? How high is the sky?

The most stunning observation made by preschool children is that a boy has a penis and a girl does not. It is a sobering fact, coming as it does at an age when sameness is fairness, and they have their own theories to explain it.

A boy, so proud of his penis, decides that his sister had a penis once, too, but it was taken away because she was bad. The logical conclusion is that if it could happen to her it could happen to him—a terrifying prospect.

The little girl, also, believes that once she had a penis but somehow she lost it, as a punishment for something she cannot remember. She is envious and jealous that her brother has something she does not.

If her mother tells her that a boy has a penis but a girl will have a baby when she grows up, that explanation carries little weight with her. Seeing is believing.

In the imagination of small children the father and the mother are models of the male and female of the human race. At four and five years, children are true romantics. The little boy proudly announces that when he grows up he is going to marry his mother. His admired father has no place in this phantasy, and so, is summarily dismissed. His father may laugh, failing to appreciate the seriousness of his son's wish. The boy adopts a charming manliness and protectiveness toward his mother, bringing her presents and showing off at every opportunity. He may try to impress her with his urinary skills, and he is certain to be extremely curious about his parents' private life. Envious that they share the same bed, he may suggest switching beds with his father.

In the meantime, the little girl has every intention of marrying her father when she grows up. She would replace her mother in a minute if she knew how. She flirts with him outrageously; she flatters him in every possible way. There is no limit to her frank exhibitionism. She sets herself up as her mother's rival—intensifying already ambivalent feelings. She cannot dismiss the scary fact that if she got rid of her mother, who would take care of her when her father was not home? This thought tends to make her less than candid. Deviousness is said to be a feminine characteristic, but what else can a little girl do?

These childhood fantasies are doomed from the outset, but it takes time before each child finally realizes that his or her wishes are just that—wishes. Sadly, reluctantly, the little boy relinquishes the mother to the father; the little girl relinquishes the father to the mother. Both want to forget their passion with its intolerable frustration and anxiety.

The painful, unrequited wishes are repressed and a blessed curtain of oblivion settles down over them. Consciously, children forget these distressing ambitions; unconsciously, they do not. Conscious memory of the early years of childhood for most people is extremely fragmentary, supported largely by family stories and photographs.

Fortunately, about this time, children face the transition from home to the first year of school. From birth they have experienced a series of separations that have progressively prepared them for existence outside the family. School is their first exposure to public life alone, and it is a major separation. It begins the public side of their lives apart from their mother, and both mother and child may weep as they part on the first day of school.

# The Art of Becoming Human

Turning their backs on the safer, cared-for days of childhood, schoolchildren are compelled to face their teachers and peers by themselves, even though they lack the means with which to protect themselves.

Who is able to speak worthily of the fullness of childhood. We can not behold the little creatures which flit about before us otherwise than with delight, nay with admiration; for they generally promise more than they perform, and it seems that nature, among the other roguish tricks that she plays on us, here also especially designs to make sport of us. The first organs she bestows upon children . . . are adapted to the nearest immediate condition of the creature, which, unassuming and artless, makes use of them in the readiest way for its present purposes. The child considered in and for itself, with its equals, and in relations suited to its powers, seems so intelligent and rational, and at the same time so easy, cheerful, and clever that one can hardly wish it further cultivation. If children grew up according to early indications, we should have nothing but geniuses; but growth is not merely development; the various organic systems which constitute the man, spring one from another, follow each other, change into each other, supplant each other, and even consume each other, so that after a time scarcely a trace is to be found of many aptitudes and manifestations of ability. Even when the talents of the man have on the whole a decided direction it will be hard for the greatest and most experienced connoisseur to declare them beforehand with confidence, although afterwards it is easy to remark what has pointed to a future.

Johann Wolfgang von Goethe
*Truth and Poetry*

# 2

# Middle Childhood
## (Six to Eleven Years)

*T*he middle years of childhood, between the ages of six and eleven, are relatively calm and matter of fact. The extraordinary intensity of early childhood is buried whole and consciously forgotten, and the turmoil of adolescence lies ahead. Small wonder that this latency period is the most likely to be remembered in adulthood as happy and generally carefree.

Enrollment in school is the first formal step of separation from home, initiated this time neither by parents nor child but by the law of the land that makes education compulsory. This requirement both intrigues and terrifies a child. The absorption into the larger life of schoolmates and teachers, people who are not members of the family, is as slow as it is inexorable.

Gone forever is the innocent, unselfconscious, spontaneous behavior that was more or less sanctioned at home and nursery school, where play was the day's main occupation. Learning in nursery school, in the sense of gaining acquired knowledge, is secondary to learning about the differences in the way people outside the family behave, and how to get along with them.

A friendly first-grade teacher helps to bridge the gap between home and school during the rather horrid transition to being a part of a throng of young children—milling around, crowding, separating, and every one a stranger. Her authority is accepted with relief, as a safe haven without the need for intimacy, and her kindness is counted upon in a crisis. She often uses games to make the learning process interesting and fun.

Small children start their education relying upon their five senses to tell them everything they need to know. But as they learn more facts they become less certain that five senses are sufficient to grasp the total meaning of an experience.

Concurrently, as children learn to read, write, and count, individual strengths and weaknesses immediately reveal themselves. After the unstructured, spontaneous life of early childhood, a youngster now is often at sharp odds with the set patterns of right and wrong in the classroom. Moreover, while the mastery of one task may bring praise, it leads nevertheless to uncertainty about the next challenge.

The first several grades confront children with more and more hard facts: that two plus two always equals four, that there is usually only one correct way to spell each word. Such dogmatic realities provoke endless questions.

Answers to those questions introduce a child to the difference between what is subjective and what is objective. He or she learns that likes and dislikes are personal opinions, as opposed to objective facts. Once this distinction is clearly grasped, objective facts acquire an especially attractive luster for some children, who may passionately pursue, proclaim, and defend them. Other children never accept this difference and never will, even as adults, much preferring their own strongly held opinions to facts.

The reward for children learning the alphabet is a demonstrable expansion of their abilities. Before their eyes they see letters become words, and words become sentences—with meaning—that can be read and written. When finally they succeed in writing down their own thoughts and feelings, their joy erases every memory of grudging effort.

After the thrill of using numbers and the pleasure of choosing stories to read to oneself, there is no turning back to the parochialism of the nursery.

Another reality that jolts girls and boys equally in the early grades is the discovery that their accomplishments are more important than their personalities. Suddenly purpose, not play, is the order of the day. Rules are to be learned and applied systematically. The teacher strikes a most grievous blow at spontaneity when she draws a clear and distinct line between work and play and enforces its observance with unremitting insistence.

In time the avid curiosity of young children finds a constructive outlet in the pursuit of facts that attract their attention, and nothing escapes that attention once their interest is aroused. Industrious and persistent, they win praise from teachers and parents alike. An alert teacher, possessed of tact and unintrusiveness, will further a child's passion for facts with helpful books.

Even more important than the knowledge a child gains from accumulated facts is understanding. In the course of a lifetime, understanding will prove far more precious than knowledge. But the first step, nonetheless, is to know. And as Spinoza pointed out, from the fact of knowing something, you know what it is to know that thing. And as many a child discovers, there is nothing more fascinating than to discover a well-known fact—all by yourself.

You may accumulate a vast amount of knowledge but it will be
of far less value to you than a much smaller amount if you

have not thought it over for yourself; because only through ordering what you know, by comparing every truth with every other truth, can you take complete possession of your knowledge and get it into your power. You can think only about what you know, so you ought to learn something; on the other hand, you can know only what you have thought about. . . .

It may sometimes happen that a truth, an insight, which you have slowly and laboriously puzzled out by thinking for yourself could easily have been found already in a book; but it is a hundred times more valuable if you have arrived at it by thinking for yourself. For only then will it enter your thought-system as an integral part and living member, be perfectly and firmly consistent with it and in accord in its other consequences and conclusions, bear the hue, color and stamp of your whole manner of thinking, and have arrived at just the moment it was needed; thus it will stay firmly and forever lodged in your mind.

> Arthur Schopenhauer
> "On Thinking for Yourself"
> *Essays and Aphorisms*

As the horizon of their world slowly but progressively expands, children instinctively gravitate toward one of two typical ways of verifying facts. Some children, those who are a bit more skeptical, feel satisfied only with what they see for themselves directly, and they cling to this method of comprehension for the rest of their lives. They will be and will feel most successful when dealing with tangible, practical, quantifiable things, like money, for instance, and will not mind being called "hands-on" people. Being strictly perceptual, they believe a fact is a fact that speaks for itself.

Goethe, who spent a lifetime with dazzling, conceptual

ideas, recalls an incident in middle childhood of clearly perceptual origin.

> Children . . . have an instinct, resembling that possessed by
> rats and mice; they watch all crevices and holes, where they
> think they may procure some forbidden dainty, and they enjoy
> it with a species of secret, stolen pleasure, which in fact forms
> the chief part of childhood's happiness. I was more expert than
> my brothers, in discovering any key which might have been
> left accidentally in its lock. The greater the reverence of my
> heart for those well-fastened doors, which I was obliged to
> pass by for weeks and months, and into which I could do no
> more than cast a furtive glance when our mother opened the
> sanctuary, to take something therefrom—the quicker was I to
> seize any opportunity which the carelessness of the house-
> keeper permitted. . . .
>
> There are few of the fancied joys of life, which equalled
> my happiness when my mother occasionally summoned me to
> assist her in carrying anything out. . . . The gathered treasures
> of the place bewildered my imagination by their variety, and
> the charming perfume exhaled from such a collection of
> spices, affected me so sensibly, that I never missed an oppor-
> tunity, when near, of inhaling the dainty atmosphere.
>
> One Sunday morning, when my mother's movements
> were hastened by the church bells, the key of this precious
> room was left in the door, whilst the whole house lay in deep
> Sabbath stillness. As soon as I made the discovery, I walked
> quietly backwards and forwards several times, till at last
> approaching softly, I opened the door, and at one step found
> myself in the presence of so many long wished for sources of
> happiness.

Johann Wolfgang von Goethe
*Wilhelm Meister's Apprenticeship*

49

Dreamier children are apt to feel more comfortable with ideas about facts. Concepts rather than perception stimulate their imagination, and throughout their lives their strengths will be conceptual. They believe that appearance alone does not take into account all that is known, experienced, or implied by objective facts. They rely heavily upon significant memories of the past to set their conceptual ideas ablaze.

> Now you can apply yourself voluntarily to reading and learning, but you cannot really apply yourself to thinking: thinking has to be kindled, as a fire is by a draught, and kept going by some kind of interest in its object, which may be an objective interest or merely a subjective one. The latter is possible only with things that affect us personally, the former only to those heads who think by nature, to whom thinking is as natural as breathing.
>
> Arthur Schopenhauer
> "On Thinking for Yourself"
> *Essays and Aphorisms*

These two radically different ways of seeing and dealing with daily life manifest themselves clearly in the early grades, and they become more pronounced as the child copes with increasingly complex ideas and situations. Both capacities are wonderful gifts. Fortunately, no child or adult is a pure example of either of these two diametrically opposite ways of comprehending reality. Inevitably, serious difficulties in understanding arise between perceptual and conceptual people, not only in childhood but throughout life, as a result of these two different ways of grasping facts.

It is enormously helpful at any age—the earlier the better—to recognize these different ways of thinking in ourselves and others. Two adults who can identify the source of their friction as a clash between perceptual and conceptual thinking are more likely to resolve serious misunderstandings. In time, with patience and tolerance, they may even be able to untangle their respective versions of the truth. It behooves conceptual people to appreciate this, and to take the first step toward a mutual understanding by narrowing their typically panoramic focus to the specifics of the here-and-now.

The expectations of the schoolroom gradually encourage each child to create a public face that masks the old familiar self. The private self still peeks out sideways at its classmates while the teacher at the head of the class strides forward and onward with the public lessons. How odd, different, and intriguing the other children are: some attractive, some repellent. The many ways they look, act, and think are amazing, even peculiar. In the earliest grades, if secure in the sovereignty of his or her own selfhood within the family, each child views the world with dispassionate curiosity and inquisitiveness.

Passion springs to life the minute school lessons are graded and children see for themselves how their work is judged. They may be frustrated or angry to learn that their performance does not match their intention. Very often the teacher has to convince them of their error, since they never knew they made one. In their distress they may look at themselves objectively for the first time—as the teacher sees them—instead of as the self that they regard as being without fault. The dialogue, thus begun between the facts of their public self and the feelings of their private self, makes them squirm and want to run away. In fact, they do run away from self-examination for as long as possible.

Inevitably, having compared their work with their intentions, they compare their work with that of their classmates. The results are often disagreeable. Envy and anger quickly arise, but sharpest by far is a secret feeling of self-righteous pride if their grade outranks their neighbors'.

# The Art of Becoming Human

After sitting still for so long in the classroom, the urgent need to run around bursts out at recess. In the rough-and-tumble play on the school playground, children learn to harden themselves, as each child discovers the meaning of a slap, a pinch, a shove. Whether one is weak or strong, physical aggression precedes the learned articulateness of verbal aggression. A child is acutely aware that the proper behavior his parents demand at home is a woefully insufficient defense against the unrestrained free-for-all of the playground.

As the children of the cultivated classes grow up, a great contradiction appears. Urged and trained by parents and teachers to deport themselves moderately, intelligently, and even wisely; to give pain to no one from petulance or arrogance, and to suppress all the evil impulses which may be developed in them; but yet on the other hand, while the young creatures are engaged in this discipline, they have to suffer from others that which in them is reprimanded and punished. In this way, the poor things are brought into a sad strait between the natural and civilized states, and after restraining themselves for a while, break out according to their characters into cunning or violence.

Force is rather to be put down by force; but a well-disposed child, inclined to love and sympathy, has little to oppose to scorn and ill-will. Though I managed pretty well to keep off the active assaults of my companions, I was by no means equal to them in sarcasm and abuse; because he who merely defends himself in such cases, is always a loser. Attacks of this sort, consequently, when they went so far as to excite anger, were repelled with physical force, or at least excited strange reflections in me, which could not be without results.

Johann Wolfgang von Goethe
*Truth and Poetry*

52

Fortunately, games offer school children a safer and happier outlet for pent-up physical energies and feelings. Free play all too often ends in a free-for-all. By contrast, the strict rules of a game divert the intense competitiveness of the players and their insatiable desire to win into acceptable channels.

By age eight or nine, children are sticklers for rules, especially if they are winning. They are fanatical in their condemnation of the faintest infraction of the rules *by others.*

More often than not, only the authority of an umpire keeps a game going; to be fair (recognizing that the same rules apply to *them*) seems not to be an innate human characteristic.

> Man's attitude toward authority . . . is a perpetual seesaw. . . .
> The infant, for the most part, accommodates itself patiently to
> the authority of parents; the boy struggles against it; the youth
> casts it off; and the man accepts it again, because experience
> has taught him that he can accomplish little without the coop-
> eration of others.
>
> Johann Wolfgang von Goethe
> *On the Theory of Color*

In sports each team values an excellent player above everything else. If a girl can hit a ball farther than a boy, the team wants her on its side in order to win. Skill outranks sex, race, color, and creed during the latency age period. Winning the game supersedes everything else.

Against the backdrop of these intense feelings and loud voices that justify, choose, compare, judge, and condemn, the teacher attempts to inculcate the art of learning to be a good loser as well as a gracious winner. Good sportsmanship has its own conventions that children can abide by only if they can control their feelings. After losing a game, there is some comfort in ventilating disappointment with classmates—misery indeed loves company—but the coach's advice is to improve their skills or accept defeat with grace.

The desire to win is so compelling that the child who begins to lose may find it very difficult to play fair—on or off the playground. Even when playing with a friend at home, cheating causes name-calling and the now "ex-friend" takes his or her belongings and marches home. Little wonder that friendship at this age is an on-again, off-again affair. Pious anger often bolsters a shaky inner code of fair play.

After school, home becomes the place where most young children run for comfort and support, and if a child lacks this refuge, it is an incalculable loss. In the early grades children share their triumphs, failures, and fears with their parents, who try to help them toughen themselves against hurt feelings and public displays of private emotions.

As children grow older they gradually share fewer confidences with their parents. Their peers become the recipients of their secrets, their companions in good and bad experiences. This transfer of confidence to friends—a separation from home of a different order—is both important and necessary. Classmates understand school and playground situations that parents can know about only secondhand. Parents, of course, do not like to feel excluded from their children's experiences, and they make every effort to keep open lines of communication. But when they ask their children pointed questions, they usually get monosyllabic answers or none at all.

Do not think the youth has no force because he cannot speak to you and me. Hark! in the next room his voice is sufficiently clear and emphatic. It seems he knows how to speak to his contemporaries. Bashful or bold, then, he will know how to make us seniors very unnecessary.

The nonchalance of boys who are sure of a dinner, and would disdain as much as a lord to do or say aught to concili-ate one, is the healthy attitude of human nature. A boy is in a parlor what the pit is in the playhouse; independent, irrespon-sible, looking out from his corner on such people and facts as pass by, he tries and sentences them on their merits in the swift, summary ways of boys, as good, bad, interesting, silly, eloquent, troublesome. He cumbers himself never about con-sequences, about interests; he gives an independent, genuine verdict. You must court him; he does not court you.

Ralph Waldo Emerson
*Essays*

Children become less concerned about what their parents think of their appearance, language, and manners than what their schoolmates think. At this time and increasing with each year, parents go through their own growth and development of tolera-tion of differences, acceptance with regret of the fad clothing and freak haircuts, the impenetrable slang, the manners difficult to accept. The fear of peer pressure to experiment with drugs and sex lies ahead. As long as these children feel that they blend in inconspicuously with their contemporaries, they are satisfied. They care less about being a credit to their parents than being a member in good standing within their peer group. They care even less that their parents want them to be different from what they are. And if their parents continually remind them of unfin-ished chores, children become impatient; they do not forget, they just prefer to act in their own sweet time.

Family confrontations make boys and girls alike feel that their parents simply do not understand them, and they soon become as critical of their parents as their parents are of them. A generation gap is in the making. Indeed, these young children are beginning to observe with wide-eyed disbelief the gaffes of their obtuse elders.

> Richest in almost incomprehensible experiences, however, were the birthdays. . . . On this day one got up with a right to joy that was not to be doubted. Probably the sense of this right had been very early developed in one, at the stage when one grasps at everything and gets simply everything. . . .
>
> But suddenly come those curious birthdays when, fully established in the consciousness of this right, one sees others becoming uncertain. . . . One hears something break as the presents are being arranged on the table in the next room; or somebody comes in and leaves the door open, and one sees everything before one should have seen it. That is the moment when something like an operation is performed on one: a brief but atrociously painful incision. But the hand that does it is experienced and steady. It is quickly over. And scarcely has it been survived, when one no longer thinks about oneself; one must rescue the birthday, watch the others, anticipate their mistakes, and confirm them in the illusion that they are managing everything admirably. They do not make it easy for one. . . .
>
> One managed all these things as they were demanded of one; it required no special ability. Talent was really necessary only when someone had taken pains and, important and kind, brought one a joy, and one saw even at a distance that it was a joy for somebody quite different, a totally alien joy; one didn't even know anyone for whom it would have done: so alien was it.

> Rainer Maria Rilke
> *The Notebooks of Malte Laurids Brigge*

Besides birthdays, the big family celebrations of Christmas and Hannukah make nearly all children restless with anticipation. There are the presents, the secrets, the fragrances coming from the kitchen, the abundance and variety of holiday sweets. Older children know that Santa Claus is an idea rather than a fact but are not quite mean enough to say so to their younger siblings, who are still true believers.

By middle childhood the inescapable fatal quality of fairy tales has lost its grip upon a child's imagination. What remains for boys and girls is a quite remarkable collection of superstitions, despite their growing respect for facts. What child will deliberately walk on a crack, however much he doubts that it will break his mother's back? Who wants to risk it, even if his mother is temporarily out of favor?

School children are profound believers in luck, and they do everything in their power to tilt the scales of fortune. Their pockets sag with a miscellany of lucky pieces. They never open umbrellas indoors or walk under ladders outdoors. Black cats are anathema; a broken mirror, a disaster. There are not enough facts to explain everything that children need to know in order to feel safe.

As children develop private lives of their own, parents try to bridge the growing separation by reminding their sons or daughters of the good times of early childhood. It seems quite extraordinary that a psychological curtain of oblivion has rung down on school children's memory of their early years. The parents' memories, expressed in stories and illustrated by family photographs, become the main source of a child's awareness of his own infancy. A child listens passively to these tales of her or his younger days, as if they had happened to somebody else. Children are only mildly interested in their earlier life; the daily happenings with their friends outside the home now claim their attention. If pressed for details about their past, they tell you to ask their mothers.

In direct contrast, the exploits, the absurdities, the mighty plans, the puny executions and hilarious naughtiness of these years become lasting memories—in fact, most often cherished in adulthood as the happy, carefree days of childhood.

When Goethe, as a young boy, had seen a wondrously beguiling puppet show that stirred his imagination, he enlisted his friends to act out their own version.

> When children play they can make something out of anything: a stick becomes a gun, a piece of wood a sword, any old bundle a doll, and any corner a hut. . . . Totally unaware of our limited abilities, we embarked on anything and everything; we never realized that we sometimes confused one character with another, and assumed that everyone would take us for what we claimed to be. . . .
>
> [If someone] showed us how to enter and exit, how to declaim, how to use gestures, he got little thanks for his pains, for we were sure that we knew more than he did. . . .
>
> Yet, all this playacting, though it lacked both understanding and direction, was not without its usefulness. We trained our memories, exercised our bodies, achieved greater ease in speaking, and greater refinement in behavior than children at that age usually acquire.
>
> Johann Wolfgang von Goethe
> *Wilhelm Meister's Apprenticeship*

Clannish as school children are, to be a member of a club, especially a secret club, is the height of bliss. Passwords and signs figure prominently in elaborate rituals, so elaborate, in fact, that the members themselves have trouble remembering them. Secrecy gives children power over the uninitiated and swells their pride in their own exclusiveness. Great envy stirs in the wistful hearts of nonmembers, especially younger ones, as they feel the door of discrimination slam shut in their faces. Race, color, creed, sex, and especially age are all factors in determining membership, which causes hurt feelings, anger, and retaliation on the part of the excluded.

"Look," John Henry said, and he was staring out of the window. "I think those big girls are having a party in their clubhouse."

"Hush!" Frankie screamed suddenly. "Don't mention those crooks to me."

There was in the neighborhood a clubhouse, and Frankie was not a member. The members of the club were girls who were thirteen and fourteen and even fifteen years old. They had parties with boys on Saturday night. Frankie knew all of the club members, and until this summer she had been like a younger member of their crowd, but now they had this club and she was not a member. They had said she was too young and mean. On Saturday night she could hear the terrible music and see from far away their light. Sometimes she went around to the alley behind the clubhouse and stood near a honeysuckle fence. She stood in the alley and watched and listened. They were very very long, those parties.

"Maybe they will change their mind and invite you," John Henry said.

"The son-of-a-bitches."

Frankie sniffled and wiped her nose in the crook of her arm. She sat down on the edge of the bed, her shoulders slumped and her elbows resting on her knees. "I think they have been spreading it all over town that I smell bad," she said. "When I had those boils and that black bitter smelling ointment, old Helen Fletcher asked what was that funny smell I had. Oh, I could shoot every one of them with a pistol."

She heard John Henry walking to the bed, and then she felt his hand patting her neck with tiny little pats. "I don't think you smell so bad," he said. "You smell sweet."

# The Art of Becoming Human

"The son-of-a-bitches," she said again. "And there was something else. They were talking nasty lies about married people. When I think of Aunt Pet and Uncle Ustace. And my own father! The nasty lies! I don't know what kind of fool they take me for."

"I can smell you the minute you walk in the house without even looking to see if it is you. Like a hundred flowers."

"I don't care," she said, "I just don't care."

"Like a thousand flowers," said John Henry, and still he was patting his sticky hand on the back of her bent neck.

Frankie sat up, licked the tears from around her mouth, and wiped off her face with her shirttail. She sat still, her nose widened, smelling herself. Then she went to her suitcase and took out a bottle of Sweet Serenade. She rubbed some on the top of her head and poured some more down inside the neck of her shirt. "Want some on you?"

John Henry was squatting beside the open suitcase and he gave a little shiver when she poured the perfume over him. He wanted to meddle in her traveling suitcase and look carefully at everything she owned. But Frankie only wanted him to get a general impression, and not count and know just what she had and what she did not have.

So she strapped the suitcase and pushed it back against the wall.

"Boy!" she said. "I bet I use more perfume than anybody in this town."

Carson McCullers
*The Member of the Wedding\**

At club meetings of eight- to ten-year-olds, most of the time is spent making rules, arguing about them, and if there is any time left over, the club members usually get into mischief.

*Excerpt from *The Member of the Wedding.* Copyright © 1946 by Carson McCullers, © renewed 1974 by Floria V. Lasky. Reprinted by permission of Houghton Mifflin Co. All rights reserved.

Rough play and even cruelty seem very funny to these children, with their broad, slapstick sense of comedy. Despite their wariness, many a cat ends up in trouble. Dogs are too compliant and unsuspecting to be worthy of torment. If someone slips and falls down, there is no more hilarious sight to them, and no thought is given to the possible injury of the victim.

Fortunately, the lifespan of these secret clubs in middle childhood is short, ending usually because of disputes that defy solution, and the utter failure of the democratic process. Compromise does not come easily to children without an adult to act as arbitrator.

The prankish, roguish element of childhood behavior would drift further toward delinquency were it not for the do's and don't's that parents preach day in and day out. A black-and-white sense of right and wrong invades a child's consciousness. Even though these children's interpretation of right and wrong is always biased by self-interest, there is a grudging awareness of what is acceptable behavior that serves as a rough guide for action. Without it, children are literally lawless.

When a child has committed an offense, however serious, hopefully his or her parents' concern and love for their child permits a process of repair to occur. To be forgiven and restored to the family circle—without character assassination—helps a child to learn to forgive himself. To discover that a wrong can be made right—if the parties concerned know how to treat each other fairly and with respect—is to experience repentance and redemption.

Very slowly, over the years, the pain of remorse after wrongdoing, followed by the balm of restitution, tempers a child's fierce feelings and erratic acts, so that the behavior he or she wants to emulate comes closer to being possible.

For many years the most successful organizations for young school children under adult leadership have been Cub Scouts and Brownies. The formal structure of these organizations keeps the group functioning despite individual differences of opinion. One of the most persuasive and appealing aspects of membership—it cannot be denied—is the uniform, which never fails to make a boy or a girl feel absolutely resplendent, even faintly anointed.

While wearing the Cub Scout or Brownie uniform, a child tries to live up to the standards of allegiance that the uniform symbolizes. The uniform plays upon their sensibilities, bringing out their very best behavior. Underneath the uniform, of course, is the same old child playing host to all sorts of tantalizing and conflicting desires. Even so, the self he or she appears to be—while wearing the uniform—has his or her full approval.

The concept of doing good works is integral to these organizations. In a burst of good will, children assist in community projects, even though their altruism has delicate and shallow roots. One day children will join a community beautification project and work hard at cleaning up trash; the very next day, during an idle afternoon, they may be the first to litter a public park.

Because children do so like to belong, they feel very happy and content, at this age, to be members of a structured and predictable community. School is the center of their lives with its many pleasurable, affirming aspects: books and ideas, team sports, sociability with classmates. Belonging to all of it is an enormous satisfaction for most children. It bestows a sublime confidence in the permanency of their daily existence. They may never again feel quite so sure of their world and their lives, unless, in late adulthood, they are so fortunate as to reclaim this human potential of belonging to and living in harmony with the people, things, and ideas that they have made their own.

The next separation that awaits these prepubescent children will shatter this notion of security, certainty, and confidence, as it plunges them into the tug of war between the glory and the despair that is adolescence.

# 3

## *Late Childhood*
## *(Twelve to Seventeen Years)*

And sure enough, it comes. The god, who once soared from the ancient wilderness up into heaven, plunges down thence towards us like a bird on airy pinions and flutters around our heads and breast all through the spring day; at times he seems to withdraw, but he returns from his withdrawal; then our anguish is delight and our tremor is sweetness. Many a heart wanders and is lost in too general a love, but the noblest devotes itself to one object alone.

Johann Wolfgang von Goethe
"First, Last Words, Orphic: Love"

Entrance into school gave children in middle childhood a public life apart from their families. Now, in adolescence, a storm brews over their rights to a private life apart from their families.

Up until this age children accept as a matter of course the proprietary rights of mothers to their immature bodies. Mothering is synonymous with protection, and it is the mother's prerogative to kiss a hurt to make it well. It is also her responsibility, recognized by both mother and child, to watch over the child, as if taking care were more her business than the child's.

But no longer! As physical maturation progresses, a boy or girl will increasingly and vigorously deny the mother's right to protect them. In the struggle for an identity apart from the family, adolescents lay vehement claim to the exclusive possession of their own bodies. The mother is rejected; the adolescent insists upon privacy to the point that he or she gradually becomes an outcast within the family circle.

The father, too, suffers rejection. His prerogatives over family decisions meet with resistance and challenge. The surge of private, personal feelings pushes an adolescent to rebel against the father's right to make choices for him. He wants, and needs, to make his own decisions, independent of family plans.

The lifelong, intimate "we" relationship, particularly with the mother, loses its validity, and in its place a self-conscious sense of single identity—of me, myself, and I—asserts itself: *I am I and the wonder is in me.*

It is a heady, scary sensation to feel separate and apart from one's family, always before the main source of support, comfort, and advice. Demanding freedom from the known means relinquishing many safe havens.

Adolescence is not planned. It happens. Admission to it is without intention, and undertaken without a guide. Its ultimate goal could not be more important: to attain the possibility of living one's own life. Each boy and girl is privately petrified by its many surprises.

Thus, at certain epochs, children part from parents, servants from masters, protégés from their patrons; and whether it succeeds or not, such an attempt to stand on one's own feet, to make one's self independent, to live for one's self, is always in accordance with the will of nature.

> Johann Wolfgang von Goethe
> *Truth and Poetry*

Adolescents want to assume full responsibility for a whole range of adult activities with which they have had little or no experience. To accede to adult privileges, adolescents discover—with growing impatience—that they have to pay more and more attention to details that they had always taken for granted. Almost the first desire is to drive the family car. Having watched their parents drive so often, they think that they can do it as well, without practice. Once behind the wheel, they find driving more difficult than anticipated. They had failed to notice and appreciate the coordination of small details. In the shift from passive observer to active participant, adolescents need considerable time to achieve smooth performance. In fact, their performance in the driver's seat of a car is so erratic that the parent in the passenger seat spends most of the lesson cringing, flinching, or shouting. Everyone's nerves are spared if the teenager turns to another adult outside of the family who can teach the necessary skills with greater objectivity.

Adolescent upheaval is not restricted to home and family; it trails along with them to school. The camaraderie, based upon performance, between boys and girls of latency age vanishes in the face of the physical and emotional vulnerabilities of adolescence. A boy may suddenly see that a girl who has been a pal and playmate all his life is the possessor of golden hair that glitters in sunlight. Such a riveting experience complicates their former matter-of-fact relationship. A girl is just as vulnerable to an unexpected awareness of the irresistible smile of one particular boy. In self-defense girls flock together with girls, and boys with boys.

# The Art of Becoming Human

The dramatic outer changes of puberty cloak the crucial inner emotional changes that expose adolescents to overwhelming new feelings and ideas about themselves and the opposite sex, creating a turmoil of fear and uncertainty, often masked by deceptive bravado.

The rough-and-tumble behavior that was acceptable to boys and girls during latency is not tolerated in adult society. Courtesies that had no previous place in their lives become necessary. Not since their preschool days does appearance and personality suddenly seem more important than successful action. The embarrassment of feeling clumsy and ill-mannered in social situations pressures teenagers to adopt more conventional behavior.

Divested of the sovereignty that came with successful performance and known approval, the adolescent is overwhelmed by expectations and desires that have no clear definition. Caught between the reality of outer, physical changes and the pressure of inner, urgent feelings, adolescents are inevitably drawn to self-examination. But daydreaming soon overtakes any serious attempt to think about the chaos in their minds—to the point that moodiness, not clarity, is frequently the result. Boys, especially, find hard physical exercise more congenial and beneficial than thought. Girls find themselves talking endlessly about trivia.

With the onset of menses a girl becomes physically mature, but emotional maturity lies considerably farther down the road. Bodily changes make her extremely self-conscious and self-critical. Girls commiserate with each other over their perceived defects, using one another as sounding boards, often listening only long enough to establish their own imagined problems as the worst. Each girl exaggerates the slightest fault, certain that no one else's burden is as heavy as her own.

The truth is that each girl for the first time in her life is confronted emotionally with experiences whose origin is internal rather than external, and with which she is ill-equipped to deal. Up until now her emotions were in direct response to the people and circumstances in her environment. Now, by some mysterious conversion, a union is being forged between her body and psyche that gives a third dimension to her reactions.

By much talking she seeks to define herself. In the words she hears herself say she seeks an explanation of herself. She talks herself into an uncertain, hazy, verbal existence, the results of which she looks at with considerable wonderment. By this means she begins to recognize what sets her apart from her friends. Although she talks continuously, she is aware that her innermost feelings are incommunicable. A glimmering recognition of something that is real—and hers alone—is beginning to form in her consciousness. Yet what she says, what she thinks, and what she feels remain in large part disconnected, waiting to be assembled into a recognizable whole.

Thus it is that an adolescent girl continues to chatter with her friends while her behavior remains skittish. From a safe distance, while literally looking down on boys her own age, she dreams about older, taller boys.

This does not make one whit of difference to the boys in her class, who are likely to herd together and raise their voices in derision of girls in general. Their shouts are far from complimentary; girls reject the words with sniffs, while hoping that the taunts are not true. Most boys in early adolescence are loud-mouthed and abrasive in a group, where there is safety and anonymity. They pretend to hate girls but the truth is that they prefer sports. Let a game, any game, start and they will immediately gravitate to it and stop pestering the girls.

A different drama awaits a boy at his sexual maturation; his sexuality has nothing to do with a monthly cycle nor is his fertility limited to a circumscribed period of years. Once established, it is his for life. To his amazement and discomfiture, as his genitals develop, the close relationship between them and his feelings and thoughts is made vividly clear by spontaneous erections during the day and nocturnal emissions at night.

It is difficult for a boy to accept the link between his body and mind. Having valued the idea of being in control of himself, he now finds that he often is not. Sexual responsiveness is ever-present, and spontaneous erections are exactly that—spontaneous. That a part of his body has a life of its own can only be greeted by him with surprise, tinged sometimes with pleasure but often with dismay and embarrassment.

Physical growth in adolescence can be disconcerting if it is too fast or too slow. Who wants to be the shortest kid on the block? A boy may leave school in June as a little boy and return in the autumn as a tall, thin, all but unrecognizable youth. He is a stranger to himself as well as to others.

Most adolescent boys are very cocky, especially in a group. They compete with each other to show off their new manliness. They act as if they are equal to any situation—a hopeful feeling, not a tested fact. With considerable high-handedness they behave as if the fact could easily be established should they deign to prove it. Indeed, an adolescent boy feels that he does not have to prove a thing—until one fine day a special girl walks straight into the center of his life.

> Bid adieu, adieu, adieu,
> Bid adieu to girlish days,
> Happy Love is come to woo
> Thee and woo thy girlish ways—
> The zone that doth become thee fair,
> The snood upon thy yellow hair.

When thou hast heard his name upon
The bugles of the cherubim,
Begin thou softly to unzone
Thy girlish bosom unto him
And softly to undo the snood
That is the sign of maidenhood.

James Joyce
"Chamber Music"*

The heart of an adolescent, boy or girl, at the beginning of sexual awakening is as tightly shut as the bud of a springtime flower. In the soft surprise of infatuation, delight and anguish bubble up spontaneously. The origin is located in the center of oneself, capable of being known but not of being explained. A sudden, secret communication between the eyes and the mind arouses a surprising wave of feeling that floods the whole consciousness. It is called love, and each lover believes that these feelings were never experienced in the world before. The heart bashfully opens to someone else and at once goes seeking—impatiently, fearfully, hopefully—for the faintest response of the beloved.

Being your slave what should I do but tend
Upon the hours and times of your desire?
I have no precious time at all to spend,
Nor services to do, till you require,
Nor dare I chide the world-without-end hour
Whilst I, my sovereign, watch the clock for you,
Nor think the bitterness of absence sour
When you have bid your servant once adieu;

---

*"Chamber Music XI, 'Bid adieu, adieu,' " from *Collected Poems* by James Joyce. Copyright 1918 by B. W. Huebsch, Inc., 1927, 1936 by James Joyce, 1946 by Nora Joyce. Used by permission of Viking Penguin, a division of Penguin Books USA Inc.

## The Art of Becoming Human

Nor dare I question with my jealous thought
Where you may be, or your affairs suppose,
But, like a sad slave, stay and think of nought
Save, where you are how happy you make those.
So true a fool is love that in your will
Though you do any thing, he thinks no ill.

William Shakespeare
Sonnet LVII

In an instant, a boy and girl pass over the threshold to the land of love and enchantment. Love, which is capable of harmonizing the most unruly feelings, has a long, long history in each person's private experience, beginning at birth and ending at death. Being loved as young children by parents, family, and friends who court them into a responding love sets a pattern of being loved first, before loving. To be loved is one thing, to be a lover quite another. To beguile one's mother at three years of age is not the same as Romeo being enamored of Juliet at thirteen years. For the first time, adolescents encounter the sexual aspects of love.

It may take a lifetime, after many painful, wonderful experiences, to begin to understand, at last, why love may border on, protect, and salute another human being, as Rilke has said, but never be possessive. There is so much to learn about love; most importantly, what it really is.

It is hard to explain scientifically, Son, he said. . . . [The science] is this. And listen carefully, I meditated on love and reasoned it out. I realized what is wrong with us. Men fall in love for the first time. And what do they fall in love with?

The boy's soft mouth was partly open and he did not answer.

A woman, the old man said. Without science, with nothing to go by, they undertake the most dangerous and sacred expe-

70

rience on God's earth. They fall in love with a woman. Is that correct, Son?

Yeah, the boy said faintly.

They start at the wrong end of love. They begin at the climax. Can you wonder it is so miserable? Do you know how men should love?

The old man reached over and grasped the boy by the collar of his leather jacket. He gave him a gentle little shake and his green eyes gazed down unblinking and grave.

Son, do you know how love should be begun?

The boy sat small and listening and still. Slowly he shook his head. The old man leaned closer and whispered:

A tree. A rock. A cloud. . . .

For six years now I have gone around by myself and built up my science. And now I am a master, Son. I can love anything. No longer do I have to think about it even. I see a street full of people and a beautiful light comes in me. I watch a bird in the sky. Or I meet a traveler on the road. Everything, Son. And anybody. All stranger and all loved! Do you realize what a science like mine can mean?

The boy held himself stiffly, his hands curled tight around the counter edge. Finally he asked: Did you ever really find that lady?

What? What say, Son?

I mean, the boy asked timidly, Have you fallen in love with a woman again?

The old man loosened his grasp on the boy's collar. He turned away and for the first time his green eyes had a vague and scattered look. He lifted the mug from the counter, drank down the yellow beer. His head was shaking slowly from side to side. Then finally he answered: No, Son. You see that is the last step in my science. I go cautious. And I am not quite ready yet.

Carson McCullers
"A Tree · A Rock · A Cloud"

# The Art of Becoming Human

The experience of most adolescents is to fall in love, an experience that is quite different from lasting love. The first time it happens is seldom the last time, nor is the object of sexual desire always a beloved. Eros is essentially impersonal; its sexuality is primarily synonymous with self-assertion, lust, and power.

Adolescent love—driven by pleasure, desire, competition, jealousy, and a host of other passions—all too often fails wretchedly in its objective. Most frequently, self-love is the greatest obstacle to being able to love another. Adolescents may not consider and certainly do not understand the feelings of their beloved at all. Or they arrogantly assume that their feelings and those of the beloved are alike. A young lover has yet to learn that no two people are alike.

> First of all, love is a joint experience between two persons—but the fact that it is a joint experience does not mean that it is a similar experience to the two people involved.
>
> There are the lover and the beloved, but these two come from different countries. Often the beloved is only a stimulus for all the stored-up love which has lain quiet within the lover for a long time hitherto. And somehow every lover knows this. He feels in his soul that his love is a solitary thing. He comes to know a new, strange loneliness and it is this knowledge which makes him suffer. So there is only one thing for the lover to do. He must house his love within himself as best he can; he must create for himself a whole new inward world—a world intense and strange, complete in himself.
>
> Let it be added here that this lover about whom we speak need not necessarily be a young man saving for a wedding ring—this lover can be a man, woman, child or indeed any human creature on this earth.

Carson McCullers
*The Ballad of the Sad Café*

Love is neither a sexual game nor a passing infatuation that can be experienced and repeated according to whim. For many people flirting, sexual attraction, and making love is a pastime, played out in a variety of ways for most of their lives. They know nothing of a natural, unerring love.

The term "natural, unerring love" is used by Dante in his *Divine Comedy* to express, as he says, an inevitability, like that of heavy bodies for the center, of fire for the circumference, or of plants for their natural habitat.

At the beginning of the history of human love, the unconscious affinity that the biblical Adam and Eve felt for each other was innocent. This innocence was destroyed, so the story goes, when they were beguiled by the serpent to eat the apple from the Tree of Knowledge. Among the first manifestations of their newly acquired knowledge were comparison, judgment, and condemnation. These responses, incompatible with the harmony of natural love said to be pervasive in the Garden of Eden, intensified the necessity for their expulsion.

For virtually all of us, privation and suffering play a prominent part in our experience of love. Each occurrence sharpens and refines the definition of who we really are, and, perhaps, helps us to understand somewhat better who the other person really is as well. To love means to be so free of self-absorption, sorrow, and hurt that we are able to see others more clearly and without projection of our own hopes and fears. The significant change in us is the replacement of our self-centeredness by a newly awakened compassion for another person. With our whole being we come upon an experience that teaches us what it is to be human.

In a flash all of the playfulness of falling in love is charged with utmost seriousness. This change shifts the focus of our lives forever. Desire that so confuses every adolescent's heart is softened and transformed into devotion.

# The Art of Becoming Human

| | |
|---|---|
| *Romeo* | Thou chid'st me oft for loving Rosaline— |
| *Friar* | For doting, not for loving, pupil mine. |
| *Romeo* | And bad'st me bury love— |
| *Friar* | Not in a grave, |
| | To lay one in, another out to have. |
| *Romeo* | I pray thee chide me not. . . . Juliet, I love now, |
| | Doth grace for grace and love for love allow. |
| | The other did not so. |
| *Friar* | O she knew well |
| | Thy love did read by rote that could not spell. |
| | But come, young waverer, come go with me, |
| | In one respect I'll thy assistant be, |
| | For this alliance may so happy prove |
| | To turn your households' rancor to pure love. |
| *Romeo* | O let us hence! I stand on sudden haste. |
| *Friar* | Wisely and slow, they stumble that run fast. |

Shakespeare
*Romeo and Juliet*
Act 2, scene 2

The rapture of being fully conscious of the otherness of someone else floods a lover's mind and heart with new thoughts and feelings. Devotion to the beloved progressively expands the limitations of a previously unwakened psyche. Age is no barrier to the quite extraordinary revelation that you are you, and a wonder is in *you,* as well as in *me,* who stands here in your shadow.

Dante first saw Beatrice, the natural unerring love of his life, when he was nine years old and she was eight. He never forgot her, and years later he celebrated that love in *The Divine Comedy.* Romeo and Juliet were thirteen years of age at their fateful meeting. But the love that causes the shift of gravity from "me" to "you" is not limited to adolescence. It can happen at any age.

74

Concurrent with the joy of love, each lover searches and explores the beloved with a passionate objectivity, and very quickly discovers differences of personality that create a gulf between them.

This unwelcome boundary—an expression of individual *daimon,* described by Socrates as the fundamental essence of each person's being—sets a limit to their love but at the same time protects and preserves the individual integrity of each. All-consuming though the desire of the lover and the beloved is to merge, the consequence would destroy the essence of their love, the unique otherness of each.

Greta Garbo portrayed the quality of this ebb and flow between lovers, showing in film after film the rapture of love in her clinging body while, at the same time, her neck and head pulled back from a complete embrace. In this poignant gesture of resistance she seems to be impressing the image of the beloved's face upon her memory forever.

The classical example of individual integrity destroyed by a seductive, ruinous intimacy is captured in the relationship of Antony and Cleopatra. Antony's passionate devotion to Cleopatra so warped his judgment as a world conqueror that when she fled—from the battle of Actium—he followed her, abandoning his loyal soldiers to the enemy, Octavian. Antony's integrity, nobility, and achievement had always before shielded him from such temptation, but when he cast them aside at Actium, defeat, disgrace, and death followed in sharp, swift order.

> *Antony*    I have offended reputation,
>             A most unnoble swerving.
>                    (Cleopatra enters . . .)
>             O, whither hast thou led me,
>                 Egypt? See,

# The Art of Becoming Human

How I convey my shame out of thine eyes
By looking back what I have left behind
Stroy'd in dishonor.

*Cleopatra*  O my lord, my lord.
Forgive my fearful sails: I little thought
You would have follow'd.

*Antony*  Egypt, thou knew'st too well
My heart was to thy rudder tied by th'strings,
And shouldst tow me after. O'er my spirit
The full supremacy thou knew'st, and that
Thy beck might from the bidding of the gods
Command me.

*Cleopatra*  O, my pardon!

*Antony*  Now I must
To the young man send humble treaties, dodge
And palter in the shifts of lowness, who
With half the bulk o' th' world play'd as I pleas'd,
Making and marring fortunes. You did know
How much you were my conqueror, and that
My sword, made weak by my affection, would
Obey it on all cause.

*Cleopatra:*  Pardon, pardon!

*Antony*  Fall not a tear, I say; one of them rates
All that is won and lost.

William Shakespeare
*Antony and Cleopatra*
Act 3, scene 9

The ability to be able to love people justly requires a long apprenticeship. Fortunately, other loves exist toward which joy guides many a young person.

There is a love that attracts a certain, select group of adolescents: the religious experience that the early Christian Church called *agape*. The rich literature of the spirit is deeply appealing to idealistic, isolated, young people.

> If life is a kind of activity and the finer the activity the finer the life, then surely contemplation, being the most excellent of all activity, both because of its worth and its permanence, is also the greatest and most distinguished life; and, I would add, the sweetest of all. For unlike sense it does not deal with the impure, false, and fickle delights arising from external images but, possessing within itself the true and eternal causes and nature of everything, it purely, truly and permanently feeds on and rejoices at that which is pure, true and permanent. I say it takes boundless joy in the boundless and, what is most important of all, being most near to the life of God, is transformed into his perfect image.
>
> Marsilio Ficino
> *Letters*

The life of Mother Teresa is a stunning demonstration of *agape*. As an adolescent, Mother Teresa gave her life and love to her God, asking only that His love be channeled back through her to help the poorest of the poor, regardless of who or where they are. She bears witness to a lifelong compassion and love that exceed the capacities of most people. Her road, extraordinarily difficult and even horrifying, makes the very existence of her way of living all the more humbling.

> Oh most wonderful intelligence of the heavenly architect! Oh eternal wisdom, born only from the head of highest Jove! Oh infinite truth and goodness of creation, sole queen of the whole universe! Oh true and bountiful light of intelligence! Oh healing warmth of the will! Oh generous flame of our heart! Illumine us, we beg, shed Your light on us and fire us, so that we

inwardly blaze with the love of Your light, that is, of truth and wisdom.

This alone, Almighty God, is to truly know You. This alone is to live most blessedly with You. Since those who wander far from the rays of Your light can never see anything clearly, they are misled and frightened by unreal shadows, as though by terrifying nightmare, and are wretchedly tormented everywhere in perpetual night. Since they alone who live zealously with You see, love, and embrace beneath Your rays those things which are true, eternal and immeasurable; they alone will regard anything limited by time or place as a shadowy dream of no importance. Thus they cannot be dislodged from the highest citadel of heavenly bliss, either by desire or fear of earthly things.

Marsilio Ficino
*Letters*

To leap from total confusion to total direction in a split second is every adolescent's fervent desire. The more desperate the need, the deeper the acceptance of help. To have a sense of freedom and ease fill all the places in one's being that were formerly choked with care is an overwhelming experience. It is, also, an experience relatively few adolescents enjoy. The intimacy of what they take to be God's love is too much for most of them, and although they may remember it forever, those who attest their love of God at this age are likely to move away from that love for years, perhaps even for the rest of their lives.

It is more congenial for most people, of any age, to love their God's visible, tangible handiwork in nature—people, animals, plants, and the inanimate features of earth, sea, and sky—than to love a concept of Him as the Invisible One. When nature and our minds unite, in poetry, for instance, we may find a compensating solace and delight.

Do you know the land where the lemon tree blossoms,
Where the golden oranges glow in the dark foliage,
A soft wind blows from the blue sky,
And the myrtle stands silent,
And the bay tree is tall.
Do you know it, perhaps? . . .
Do you know the mountain and its cloudy path,
The mule picks its way through the mist,
In caves the ancient brood of dragons live,
The rock-face falls sheer
And the stream rushes over it.
Do you know it, perhaps?

Johann Wolfgang von Goethe
"The Minstrel"

Spared, yet awhile, from the steep, narrow way of earning a livelihood that absorbs so much time in later life, adolescents are free to look around unhurriedly at the world. The diamond glitter of sunlight on the early morning dew of a cobweb does not escape their notice. A wondering curiosity about the stars, the puzzle of the universe, the strange, rare occurrence of a blue moon, set many an adolescent's imagination on fire. This is the time to dream big dreams. Nature is so close and intimate; they, so unencumbered in their looking, so free to act according to its promptings. For some it leads directly to the lyricism of sound, color, and words; the poetic heart of adolescence is in its ascendency.

To find a means of expression for these ardent thoughts and feelings is the concern of every artist, including the adolescent artist. Serious, personal answers must be given to the questions: What is your love? What is your treasure? What is your bliss?

Almost every young person needs a guide, a model, a beacon to give a sense of direction, a sense of meaning, to his experience. Even the genius of Goethe, as a young man, needed a steadying, sympathetic mentor. In Strasbourg, he met Johann Gottfried Herder, a theologian and an original, profound thinker whose ideas exerted a lasting influence on Goethe:

> I worked with the intention of consulting you. I know that your judgment will not only open my eyes about this piece [*Goetz von Berlichingen*], but, moreover, will teach me how to regard this work as a milestone from where I have to enter upon a long, long itinerary, and in hours of rest I then may find out how far I will still have to go. Nor shall I undertake any alteration before I hear your voice, for I well know that then a radical regeneration must take place, if it is to see the light.

Johann Wolfgang von Goethe
Letter to J. G. Herder
End of 1771

Help surrounds anyone free enough to let it come to him. It is characteristic of an adolescent to seek instruction and advice rather than to let life come to him and, by being quiet and attentive, to learn from his own experience. This way of living demands the courage to take one's own thoughts and feelings seriously, despite others' attempts to shoot down one's final conclusions.

> When the soul of man is born in this country, there are nets flung at it to hold it back from flight. You talk to me of nationality, language and religion. I shall try to fly by those nets.

James Joyce
*A Portrait of the Artist as a Young Man*

As adolescence with its way of living in the moment is left behind, almost all young people rush excitedly to take up the activities that they have charted for themselves outside of the family. The public aspect of their lives is beginning—to be lived in a world dominated by the clock. Will public demands harmonize with their private lives, the realm of their loves? In their eagerness, their enthusiasm, they assume so. Life and love become their rallying cry.

Away! Away!

The spell of arms and voices: the white arms of roads, their promise of close embraces, and the black arms of tall ships that stand against the moon, their tale of distant nations. They are held out to say: We are alone—come. And the voices say with them: we are your kinsmen. And the air is thick with their company as they call to me, their kinsman, making ready to go, shaking the wings of their exultant and terrible youth. . . .

Mother is putting my new secondhand clothes in order. She prays now, she says, that I may learn in my own life and away from home and friends what the heart is and what it feels. Amen. So be it. Welcome, O life! I go to encounter for the millionth time the reality of experience and to forge in the smithy of my soul the uncreated conscience of my race. . . .

Old father, old artificer, stand me now and ever in good stead.

James Joyce
*A Portrait of the Artist as a Young Man*

# 4

# *Early Adulthood (Eighteen to Forty Years)*

C hance plays a large role throughout life, but, perhaps, never more so than in early adulthood. The people they meet, the opportunities that come their way, the state of the economy, the extent to which the world is at war or at peace—all these conditions are particularly momentous for young adults. Not only do such events profoundly affect the external circumstances of their lives, they are also beyond their personal control.

The lifelong, recurring theme of separation, with its sequel of loss, dependence, initiative, and independence, is reenacted once again during early adulthood in possibly its most dramatic form since birth.

By eighteen years of age departure from home usually is negotiated with the cooperation and approval of parents. Young people want to be independent, yet the unknown makes them uncertain, and the separation from home is often stressful. For some it is comforting to know that they can go home again, if they want to or need to, even if they return as adults rather than as children.

# The Art of Becoming Human

Most young people leave home—to attend college, begin work, join the armed forces—with high hopes, abounding friendliness, inexpressible uncertainties, enormous energy and brashness, untapped possibilities, and mostly vague plans for the future. They are available, opportunistic, brimming over with ideas and haunted by deep, indistinct, unspecified yearnings. The magnitude of their ignorance is matched only by the extravagant waste of their energies until in time they learn to focus their activities.

Away from home many will share board and room with one or more people of their own age, signaling a tentative independence, even if their parents continue to lend financial support. During this transition safety in numbers is still the rule. In high school they relied upon a close group of friends while seeking a psychological separation from their family; in college, the armed forces, or the workplace, geographical separation from home inclines them to form friendships quickly and to join their friends in all-consuming interests and activities. En masse and somewhat arrogantly, they consider anyone over thirty suspect, lacking any awareness of just how quickly they themselves will reach that very age.

It will always be true that new situations call for the protection, help, and comfort of a sponsor. But once oriented and feeling more secure, young people begin to initiate independent ideas that may be at variance with those of their sponsor, at which point they must either capitulate or separate.

Every bird has its decoy, and every man is led and misled in a way peculiar to himself. . . . I had indeed boldness enough to undertake something uncommon and perhaps dangerous, and many times felt disposed to do so; but I was without the handle by which to grasp and hold it.

Johann Wolfgang von Goethe
*Truth and Poetry*

84

The question of how to become a human being is not likely to be high on the list of priorities of most twenty-year-olds; they are too exhilarated by the glitter of daily happenings. About all they can manage is to keep their emotional reactions to the day's encounters under as much control as possible. But even if they do ask the question, they may confuse being a member of the human race with being a human being, or, more likely, they are unsure about how or where to begin.

They know where they have come from and how they feel at any given moment, but they still have much to learn about who and what they are. Of course, they think that they know—and certainly their parents, among others, have tried to tell them— but the fact remains that they do not see themselves objectively. They lack an inner vision of their own ongoing thoughts, feelings, and ideas. They are content and, in fact, quite smug, spouting second-hand opinions. They create an image of themselves that they believe quite sincerely to be the truth.

This self-image has a fleeting, chameleonlike quality. Many times they set their course due north with determination and conviction, only to arrive at a place due south, having changed direction in midstream with equal determination and conviction. Their colorful decisions are much more likely to be based on quick, impulsive feeling than on thoughtful reasoning. It is a paradox that at the very time they are so full of themselves their eyes are focused almost exclusively on the world outside.

The early twenties are chaotic because young adults' outer and inner vision are neither joined nor coordinated. All too many adventures during this early period of their lives are the result of poor planning or no planning, and as they look back at those days they may be glad that not all of their private, inappropriate acts have had public consequences. In fact, they are right to marvel at their physical survival in many situations. Standing on an apartment roof one rainy night in Paris, a young man and woman dared each other to jump the space separating them from the roof of the next building. They did and lived to wonder about their youthful exuberance that smothered all sense of prudence.

In his autobiography, Goethe writes of a painful episode in his early youth.

> I had lost that unconscious happiness of wandering about unknown and unblamed, and thinking of no observer, even in the greatest crowds. . . . [I went] into the woods, and while I shunned the monotonous firs, I sought those fine leafy groves, which do not indeed spread far in the district, but are yet of sufficient compass for a poor wounded heart to hide itself.
>
> Johann Wolfgang von Goethe
> *Truth and Poetry*

A more serious and public situation occurs when Shakespeare's Prince Hal becomes King Henry V at the death of his father, and repents of his riotous behavior with Falstaff.

*Prince*     And princes all, believe me, I beseech you; . . .
The tide of blood in me
Hath proudly flowed in vanity till now:
Now doth it turn and ebb back to the sea,
Where it shall mingle with the state of floods
And flow henceforth in formal majesty.

> William Shakespeare
> *King Henry IV, Part 2*
> Act 5, scene 2

For young people in their twenties, the springtime of life arrives, and the voice of the turtle is heard in the land. Most of them are very attractive physically, whether they see themselves that way or not, with the marvelous strength and litheness of a young body. Life is in full flood and they are swept up exuberantly by its booming tides. At every turn the sexual attractions of other young adults are likely to be overwhelming. It is a time of action, not reflection. The impulse to say a sudden yes to new, exciting experiences may well silence all promptings of caution or prudence or moderation.

Their individual personalities, composed of heredity, upbringing, education, circumstance, and habit are brought to bear on whatever they undertake. All of them have personal mannerisms that distinguish their way of doing things, their way of moving physically or standing still, their way of reacting emotionally to stress or pleasure. These traits are as much a part of them as their handwriting or their fingerprints. How they perform a task, of course, can be improved or refined, but their *daimon* will always determine why they feel more comfortable doing something one way rather than another.

Consider silent film star Charlie Chaplin, whom no one has surpassed in classical comedy. He was as decided, ready, and adroit in his movements as a hawk in the air. But behind the formidable technique, the method, the discipline that rendered complicated things simple, was a *daimon* that did not need instruction, doing what was right instinctively, naturally, and surely.

Unconscious traits of natural talent and ability—the manifestations of *daimon*—are readily recognizable by others, but young persons may not appreciate that an awareness of their instinctive style is extremely valuable information. J. D. Beazley, the eminent scholar of Greek vase painting, once said that he was brought up to think of "style" as a sacred thing, as the man himself. But too often, in fact, young adults are more likely to dismiss their special way of doing things as unworthy of comment—

unless they happen to be using their young bodies as athletes, dancers, or warriors. Those who devotes themselves to training the body to peak condition will discover that the body has its own intelligence. Indeed, their mastery may become so refined that, in Spinoza's terms, they know what it is to know the body's potential and in that moment of perfect harmony render the impossible possible. Such awareness brings with it a revelation about oneself. It is a transcendental, transforming experience.

There are other determinations of a conscious variety that subtly reflect the inner being. What kind of people, ideas, and things does one find attractive? Why is "this" more appealing than "that"? Individual choices are seldom recognized as a mirror reflection of one's nature, for attention is focused on the choice, not the chooser. Others observing from the sidelines very often see young people better than they see themselves.

The widening horizons that college offers to young adults cannot possibly be quantified. The people they meet there exert an extraordinary influence upon their lives. Some of these people need not even be alive. Usually, though, it takes a living teacher to bring to life someone long dead whose ideas and insights radically change one's understanding. Students are swept up by the moving force of thoughts that are subject to neither time nor fashion, to words whose vibrancy captures their attention, to writers who change their lives and become their friends. They do not merely read them, they learn them by heart and make them an integral part of their lives.

> Much have I travell'd in the realms of gold,
> And many goodly states and kingdoms seen;
> Round many western islands have I been
> Which bards in fealty to Apollo hold.

Oft of one wide expanse had I been told
That deep-brow'd Homer ruled as his demesne;
Yet did I never breathe its pure serene
Till I heard Chapman speak out loud and bold:
Then felt I like some watcher of the skies
When a new planet swims into his ken;
Or like stout Cortez when with eagle eyes
He star'd at the Pacific—and all his men
Looked at each other with a wild surmise—
Silent, upon a peak in Darien.

John Keats
"On First Looking Into Chapman's Homer"

Such private experiences, under the best of circumstances, may lead to other people who have had the same response. Bound together by a shared love and admiration for anyone, living or dead, who has awakened these feelings, they often become fast friends.

Who hears me, who understands me, becomes mine, a possession for all time. Nor is nature so poor but she gives me this joy several times, and thus we weave social threads of our own, a new web of relations....

Ralph Waldo Emerson
"Friendship"

It is possible, of course, to go through one's formal education untouched by such experiences. There are many who see the past—and the present, for that matter—only in terms of facts to be collected and displayed for other people's admiration and envy. To those who see life this way, everything is quantitative, therefore everything can be exploited for one's own purpose.

But those young adults who are caught by the moving force

that blows through the hearts and minds of poets, philosophers, and heroes become increasingly aware of that same moving force within their own hearts and minds. They see life in a qualitative way that makes their actions in the here and now spontaneous and alive.

Most college students are less indifferent intellectually to academic pursuits than they were in high school, for they have greater choice in what they may study. Their interests and ambitions are becoming better defined as they begin to prepare themselves for a specific career or vocation; their initiative may be valued and encouraged by college professors or other mentors who respect their emerging intellectual independence. Such benevolent scrutiny of their personal creativity in their classwork is enormously supportive and confirming. It strengthens them and contributes significantly to the growth of what is most vital in them.

Graduation from college precipitates a separation as momentous as leaving home. Some young adults elect to pursue a professional career that requires graduate training. This choice only postpones for a few more years the departure from academic life. When the time comes, entrance into the working world brings the challenge of a full-time job along with the satisfaction of earning a salary. Many graduate students are aware of the financial necessity for this day to arrive, but the day itself often carries with it an unexpectedly exquisite flavor of its own reaching far beyond necessity. They discover that economic independence is enormously enjoyable, providing as it does the means for satisfying their needs and desires.

The office building, the hospital, the museum, the marketplace, wherever the place of work may be, becomes the focal point of the young adult's life. Fellow workers on a job are not all the same age. The former college student may have the great good fortune of becoming friendly with an older, wiser colleague, kind enough to help save him from blatant error. But when he begins to feel more confident of his increasing skills, initiative and growing independence once again spring to life, and with impatient eagerness he pursues the rewards of fame, fortune, and sex.

At this stage of development young people in their twenties are in serious jeopardy. They risk becoming self-satisfied. They may lose all sense of shame and delicacy if nothing is sacred to them anymore.

> My salad days,
> When I was green in judgment,
> Cold in blood,
> To say as I said then.
>
> William Shakespeare
> *Antony and Cleopatra*
> Act 1, scene 5

Often they live lives of excess if not chaos, cloaking disorder under the hard surface of a smiling facade. They are navigating a dangerous, tortuous, swift, treacherous channel, blinded by the gleam of gold, seduced by the sweetness of success, and often gratified by easily obtained sex. Under such circumstances they are most fortunate if a voice within them, on some dark night, begins to ask questions: Why am I so exhausted and drained by this so-called success? If this is all that my life amounts to, what makes it worth living?

This self-examination may signal the first birth pains in becoming a human being. Pain, and often defeat, may offer salvation from the claims and confines of the *thou-shalt* world, as well as the *I-will* determination of blind ambition.

# The Art of Becoming Human

We, ignorant of ourselves,
Beg often our own harms, which the wise powers
Deny us for our good: so find we profit
By losing of our prayers.

William Shakespeare
*Antony and Cleopatra*
Act 2, scene 1

Such experiences reveal to young adults that the choices they make have far-reaching consequences and wield tremendous power in their lives.

If they are fortunate enough to be overtaken by love at this juncture, tact and consideration do return. Love may save them quite wondrously from their self-conceits, giving a new order and substance to their disorderly existence. The living force of another person's being can penetrate their self-absorption and set their hearts on fire. By some miracle many find a special person—longed for, even prayed for—to whom they want to commit their lives, either in marriage or in the establishment of a lasting relationship. They pull back from their group of friends to embrace the exclusive pleasure that two people find in each other. This love can dramatically increase their vitality, strength, and fruitfulness.

And my spirit, that now so long a time had passed, since trembling in her presence, it had been broken down with awe.

Without having further knowledge by mine eyes through hidden virtue which went out from her, felt the mighty power of ancient love.

Dante Alighieri
*The Divine Comedy, Purgatorio*
Canto 30

Marriage is not one life being added to another to make a twosome; rather, each partner makes some sacrifice of selfhood to create a new oneness, different from either one alone, not unlike two eggs making one omelet, as Joseph Campbell expresses it. When such an understanding of marriage is reached, loyalty and devotion are accorded to the marriage rather than to the partner, which helps marriages survive the stresses that each partner's ego places upon the relationship.

Marriage is not a love affair. It is a family affair, more, at times, like an extremely severe trial to be endured with all of its pain and turmoil. Yet, it is in marriage that people encounter one of the most deeply absorbing experiences in being alive—subordinating the instinct of self-preservation to an overwhelming desire to please and help another. All individual purposes can become secondary to this singularly passionate commitment.

Concern and compassion for another person contribute from a new quarter to the growth of who one really is. Paradoxically, as men and women curb their own self-interest by becoming keenly aware of the other, a new freedom and private joy become a part of their experience. It may, at times, feel like heaven.

Harmony in marriage, unfortunately, is fragile, more often the exception rather than the rule. After repeated efforts, leading only to more and more serious misunderstandings, the partners in a marriage may not achieve a viable union because one or both lack the resources or the grace. Perhaps they suffer from a basic incompatibility obscured by the first blossoming of their mutual attraction. In any event, it may become more and more plain that the marriage is failing. Divorce is often the only solution, even though its necessity is one of the most wrenching experiences in life, since it marks the end of a venture begun with promise.

# The Art of Becoming Human

There comes an end to passion
When the me of we cries out, "Enough."
There comes an end to passion
When the dark of you obscures the light of me.
There comes an end to passion
When the shadow of our death drifts off into space
Oh, take back me from we
Oh, take back me from we
There has to be a me to ever love again.

(Work in progress)

It is possible to take back me from we. It is possible—even though a divorce is like the killing of a song—to heal the lesion of a fractured marriage. It is even possible for some to make an enduring marriage later on. But whether the couple remarry or not, the failed marriage may be recognized in time as a very significant maturing experience.

In more stable marriages, the wish for children becomes an option played out against the calendar of the childbearing years. The idea of pregnancy and the fact of pregnancy are worlds apart. The fact is a secret at first shared by the parents and the physician, early signs being hidden and the fact digested by the mind long before the body bears visible witness. The mystery, the pride, the awe, and the fearsome omnipotence of the accomplished act hover wordlessly, radiantly, over them: the blissful consciousness of bearing a new life within oneself, as noted psychoanalyst Karen Horney expressed it. These many strands of emotion are woven into that tough fabric of parenthood so vital in keeping a family intact.

Parenthood, never easy, can be exhaustingly difficult, especially if the father and mother are pursuing active careers. No one realizes at first that raising a child draws upon all available resources, and calls for many that are in very short supply. For some it becomes unmanageable; the stresses and strains of family life put a severe burden upon the marriage, which may collapse under its weight.

A child is inordinately sensitive to tension between his parents. His life depends upon them and his instinct of self-preservation is readily affected. He will do anything to keep them together, to prevent the deep anguish that awaits him if there is a divorce. Even in those unhappy marriages that do not break up, the children are never at rest. A disproportionate amount of their energy is consumed by fear whenever their parents quarrel. Parents who think that the children do not know of their conflicts are wrong. Children know. They want desperately to be peacemakers.

It is an exception to the rule today for children to experience firsthand the joys, and stresses, of having a full-time mother at home. They accept part-time parenting with reluctance and varying degrees of protest. All too frequently, the working day begins on a distressing note for both children and parents owing to this enforced separation. There is no satisfactory solution.

It is the parent's hope that in time the children will outgrow their distress. They don't. To children, parents are always significant. Their first family will remain first to them, regardless of life's twists and turns, until they establish a first family of their own.

Parents are not blind to the fact that they are overwhelmed by their responsibilities. But as long as they labor under the illusion that they can do everything successfully, change or improvement is impossible. Often they intend to win, even if they are not quite sure what it is that they are winning. Ambition, vanity, and economics narrow the choices. Quantity, not quality, matters most in the fast lane.

Some companies acknowledge the pressures under which parents of young families work by offering them appropriate benefits. Maternity leave may replace a dismissal, even though the "mommy track" more often than not curtails a woman's progress toward the executive suite. A father, too, may be offered a paternity leave that allows him to stay home for a specified period after the birth of his child.

As families become more and more dependent upon two incomes, many women work even in the ninth month of their pregnancy. One woman was reported as saying, "I love it when the baby kicks, but, for the few minutes that it lasts, I'm not at my peak."

Recognizing the family needs of women and men in the workforce, some companies are setting up experimental nurseries and day-care facilities for the children of their employees. How successful these arrangements will be remains to be seen, for the bonding of a child to his parents, especially his mother, is not a factor to be ignored. A happy lunch hour is a boon for parents and child, but afterwards the pang of separation faces them again. It is a well-known fact that on a hospital's pediatric ward, the tears and inconsolable wails of children at the end of afternoon visiting hours can be assuaged somewhat only by serving an early supper. What other comfort is left for the children at the workplace nursery who have had their cake and eaten it, too?

For people in their thirties, there may be promotions or job changes, changes that bring more mobility, adjustments, and challenges into already overflowing lives. The fast lane is becoming faster. Even vacations, while exciting and interesting, are often far from restful. Status and prominence with their tangible rewards are the symbols of success.

As they pass the halfway point of early adulthood, most adults are living an extremely busy, exhausting, interesting life with or without children. Nietzsche has said that life at this juncture is like that of a camel:

What is heavy? so asketh the load-bearing spirit; then kneeleth it down like a camel and wanteth to be well laden.

What is the heaviest thing, ye heroes? asketh the load-bearing spirit, that I may take it upon me and rejoice in my strength.

Friedrich Nietzsche
*Thus Spake Zarathustra*

All the details of existence are piled high on their backs. Fortunately, youth supplies the strength and energy to carry heavy burdens.

The men and women who choose to follow the time-honored path of marriage and family lose certain individual freedoms, but are compensated by seeing good results grow from their labors. Eventually nesting instincts and career are brought into some kind of workable relation, buttressed by the hope that everything will fit together somehow.

A family is a unit, but it is not isolated. It is surrounded by other families, making up a neighborhood in which mutual problems and pleasures are shared. Young adults usually learn from their own experience that good fences make good neighbors— just as their grandparents and the neighbor in Robert Frost's poem told them. Their children may join with the children of their neighbors to form relationships in which the parents frequently participate. As children grow so do their community activities. Many parents discover that there is not enough time for everything; their professional meetings and business commitments are on a collision course with their children's school and extracurricular activities.

The family is a private society into which its members pour their daily experiences and reactions to each other and to other people encountered at work, school, or play. The family hears all about it. Each family has more or less active participants, with an occasional member who stubbornly keeps his own counsel, watching and listening silently. Paul Gauguin, the artist, became so stifled by the confines of family that he left his and sailed to Tahiti to paint.

Then there is the quiet sort of young adult who quits before he starts, having suffered so much from the intrusiveness of his first family that he or she never wants to start another one. That person keeps a large part of himself private and does not enter fully into any time-honored, public path.

Looking back over his long life, Goethe spoke of his experience with the endless opposition that faces youthful dreams and the need to persevere:

> Antagonists as a race . . . never become extinct. Their number, he said, is legion . . . [they] differ from me in their views and modes of thought . . . among a thousand men, you will scarce find two, who harmonize entirely in their views and ways of thinking. This being allowed I ought less to wonder at having so many opponents, than at having so many friends and adherents. My tendencies were opposed to those of my times, which were wholly subjective, while in my objective efforts, I stood quite alone to my own disadvantage. . . . I went quietly on in my own way, not troubling myself further about success, and taking as little notice as possible of my opponents.

> Johann Wolfgang von Goethe
> *Conversations with Eckermann*
> April 14, 1824

Such independent young people follow a different path. They are not dropouts in the sense of having failed or lost their way. They refuse to conform to the "thou-shalts" of society. Spurred on by their initiative to create an independent life of their own choosing, they trust themselves to survive in uncharted country. They recognize and accept as a most treasured possession their own *daimon* and want nothing more than to find the means for its expression, even if it entails a life of marginal economic certainty.

Independent spirits do not seek a sponsor, though they are grateful if they encounter someone whom they respect, who understands what they are trying to do.

The German writer Johann Peter Eckermann found in Goethe someone who understood him and whose counsel he valued deeply.

It is a great folly to hope that other men will harmonize with us; I have never hoped this. I have always regarded each man as an independent individual, whom I endeavor to study and to understand with all his peculiarities, but from whom I desired no further sympathy.

In this way have I been enabled to converse with every man, and thus alone is produced the knowledge of various characters and the dexterity necessary for the conduct of life. For it is in the conflict with natures opposed to his own that a man must collect his strength to fight his way through, and thus all our different sides are brought out and developed, so that we soon feel ourselves a match for every foe.

> Johann Wolfgang von Goethe
> *Conversations with Eckermann*
> May 2, 1824

When a vision of something larger and more compelling than personal comfort and security is acted upon, then one lives life on one's own terms. One gathers strength from one's commitment to it. It awakens a radiance of feeling fully alive, creative, and productive. This exhilarating state of mind teaches each person to pay attention to what makes her or him happy and to be faithful to it.

## 5

# Middle Adulthood
# (Forty to Sixty Years)

*I*t is high noon when men and women are in their forties, the halfway point of their lives. Everything they have been preparing for in a worldly sense has arrived, has not arrived, or, as they begin to suspect, may never arrive.

At this age people are full-fledged members of the hustling-bustling world, the madding crowd, no longer on the outside looking in but on the inside looking out. They know what they have—a job, a family, a social life, a neighborhood—and it is fortunate if it is what they want.

By middle adulthood both women and men have a better idea of who they are. They may have a professional title—doctor, lawyer, merchant, chief—and they know how they got to be where they are. But their understanding of what they are—an appreciation of the uniqueness of their private vision, their feelings, thoughts, and ideas—may remain obscure.

They may not yet have resolved the conflict between what they should do and what they would do. Unable to see themselves objectively, they plunge quickly into action. All too frequently they attempt to master anxiety by activity that in the end may become a source of pride.

Action is commendable in a dangerous situation, such as a fire, but in less pressing circumstances, it is useful to pause before acting: to think about all aspects of the public situation as well as to give uncritical, free-floating attention to private inner feelings, no matter how contrary and unacceptable. Some people may even learn to see the outer situation and their inner reactions to it so clearly that, without rancor or condemnation, they can let the matter drop; no other action is necessary. What a surprise this discovery can be.

> I know not of aught in the world that so profits a man as taking good counsel with himself; for even if things fall out against one's hopes, still one has counseled well, though fortune has made the counsel of none effect: whereas if a man counsels ill and luck follows, he has gotten a windfall, but his counsel is none the less silly.
>
> Herodotus
> *History of the Greek and Persian War*

There remains so much to learn about oneself. An inflated self-image or even an unfairly devalued one—evident, usually, only to oneself—will continue to be each person's truth until self-understanding improves. Life has already taught many worldly lessons. With experience gained by constantly confronting and coping with new situations, second-hand opinions become less attractive. The line between what women or men can do alone and what they wish to discuss with another becomes clearer. Adults are less wasteful of their energies, and more selective and sharply focused about their immediate, everyday goals.

Both sexes are changing physically. The long, lean, youthful bodily lines of early adulthood have filled out, not necessarily to middle-aged rotundity but inescapably to a recognizable maturity. To be in full flower tends to mask the fact that one is beginning to slow down a little physically, or that the marvelous strength of youth is beginning to wane, almost imperceptibly at first, yet undeniably. Even those young people who take care of their bodies with proper nutrition and exercise are likely to find doubles in tennis more appealing and less exhausting than singles. New names in the performing arts and in athletics are replacing long-admired stars. At this age, people realize that future success does not lie in the continued strength of their bodies, even though physical appearance and well-being remain important.

There is, fortunately, no decline in their emotional life. Fewer chance happenings occur because they are better planners, but their feelings are usually more intense in that they are less scattered. Fascination with the glittering surface of life recedes, replaced by a deep attraction and attachment to specific people, things, and purposes. Ambitions remain. If someone runs a race and wins a trophy, success sharpens the taste for competition. If successes multiply, these accomplishments attract the attention of powerful brokers. At first, surprised and flattered by the attention, those who are successful may begin to expect it, enamored of their own prowess.

The intense competition typical of the marketplace creates a breeding nest of pride, envy, and anger, from which violence can erupt. Dante spoke of this violence as perverse love:

> Perverse love must consist in taking a delight in evils that befall others. The proud man desires to excel and, therefore, rejoices in defeating the attempts of others. The envious man hates being overshadowed and made to think meanly of himself and his belongings and, therefore, rejoices in the misfor-

tunes of others. The angry man wishes in his indignation to make those who have offended him smart and, therefore, finds a satisfaction in their sufferings.

Dante Alighieri
*The Divine Comedy, Purgatorio*
Canto 14

To be so fortunate as to be able to free oneself from this malignant self-centeredness—the cause of perverse love—and to escape from the wretched toll of emotional energy consumed in its behalf, as well as the time wasted in plots of vengeance, is a victory worth celebrating.

In middle adulthood the people who in youth sought to create an independent life of their own and trusted themselves to survive in uncharted country are likely to continue on the trail of their adventure. The satisfaction that comes from the process of learning how to use their tools and talents well is their best reward. They want to compete only with themselves in improving their performance and to be less tempted by the self-centeredness of perverse love.

Glad as people may or may not be about where they are in their forties, many individuals begin to suffer from a growing restlessness, not unlike cabin fever. The old yearning to separate from the familiar, to explore, to investigate new ideas, to initiate, to innovate, to become independent resurfaces. A moment comes when the daily requirements that have brought so much success and recognition become unbearable. Routine is wearing them out. Compliance with daily demands is turning them into robots; talents are oppressed by outer necessity and they feel stifled.

Questions keep arising: "Is this all there is to the dreams I have dreamt?" "Isn't there something else that I am missing?" "Am I to spend the rest of my life doing nothing but this?" Nietzsche's heavy-laden camel is asking these questions and demanding clearer answers.

> But in the loneliest wilderness happeneth the second metamorphosis: here the spirit becometh a lion; freedom will it capture, and lordship in its own wilderness . . . for victory will it struggle with the great dragon.
>
> What is the great dragon which the spirit is no longer inclined to call Lord and God? "Thou-shalt" is the great dragon called. But the spirit of the lion saith, "I will."
>
> "Thou-shalt" lieth in its path, sparkling with gold—a scale-covered beast; and on every scale glittereth golden, "Thou-shalt."
>
> The values of a thousand years glitter on those scales, and thus speaketh the mightiest of all dragons: "All values of things—glitter on me.
>
> "All values have already been created, and all created values—do I represent. Verily, there shall be no 'I will' any more." Thus speaketh the dragon.
>
> My brethren, wherefore is there need of the lion in the spirit? Why sufficeth not the beast of burden, which renounceth and is reverent?
>
> To create new values—that, even the lion, cannot yet accomplish: but to create . . . freedom for new creating—that can the might of the lion do.
>
> To create . . . freedom, and give a holy Nay even unto duty: for that, my brethren, there is need of the lion.
>
> To assume the ride to new values—that is the most formidable assumption for a load-bearing and reverent spirit. . . . It once loved "Thou-shalt": now is it forced to find illusion and arbitrariness even in the holiest things, that it may capture freedom from its love: the lion is needed for this capture.

Friedrich Nietzsche
*Thus Spake Zarathustra*

# The Art of Becoming Human

How can they go on being obedient, heavy-laden camels? Something must change the status quo. The camel must become a lion, but how?

In the workplace, a common solution is a promotion, which automatically confers authority, thus avoiding a vehement quarrel with the "thou-shalt" dragon. A larger scope of activities may give all the freedom necessary for new creating.

Promotions usually are too slow for the ambitious, "successful" entrepreneur who has long since broken loose from the "thou-shalt" dragon to assert freedom with a loud, challenging "I will."

Not everyone, of course, wants to escape from the safety and prestige of a dutiful life. There are many Mr. Babbitts. Some people fear independence and are better suited to being second in command. Among them are those who do not carry within themselves the sting of unsatisfied desire, who are content with a more modest place in the programmed scheme of things, and who are obedient without loss of dignity. The root of the word *obey* (Latin: *obedire, ob-audire*) is to hear.

But few people escape the "thou-shalt" dragon without a long, painful struggle. They usually have to do something drastic about it. Goethe did twice: first, when he escaped to Weimar, and later, when he escaped from Weimar.

Before Goethe went to Weimar the publication of his novel *The Sorrows of Young Werther* brought him instant fame. He found the acclaim hollow, adding nothing to him as a human being. In fact, its high cost made him exclaim, "Oh, how often I have cursed those foolish pages of mine which made my youthful sufferings public property." Weimar offered him a welcome escape from celebrity, putting in its place a responsible reality.

Indulged as a boy and youth by his family, this gifted, lively, delightful young man found in Weimar a Grand Duke, ten years younger than himself, who was even more indulged. At first they shared the pleasures of the moment unreservedly, but in time it became incumbent upon Goethe to assume responsibility for both of them.

For ten years Goethe worked with distinction as Minister of State for Agriculture, Horticulture, and Mining, which left him little time for reflection. His success as a civil servant in the Weimar court robbed him of time to write, paint, and conduct scientific experiments.

A day came when he could bear it no longer. He disappeared, abandoning all of his administrative burdens, social obligations, and confining relationships. Months later, he wrote to his friends in Weimar of his safe arrival in Rome, where he lived for the next two years.

> At last, I have arrived in the First City of the world . . . I am convinced that the many treasures I shall bring back with me will serve both myself and others as a guide and an education for a lifetime. . . . Now that I have arrived I have calmed down and feel as if I had found a peace that will last my whole life. Because, if I may say so, as soon as one sees with one's own eyes the whole, which one hitherto had only known in fragments and chaotically, a new life begins.
>
> Johann Wolfgang von Goethe
> *Italian Journey*
> November 1, 1786

There, in Rome, free from his external "thou-shalts," Goethe sought to establish his own inner freedom by pursuing the interests that were essential to his existence. His letters home show his struggles and his resolution to achieve it:

# The Art of Becoming Human

Every day I cast off a new skin and hope to return as a human being. I shall not say how the scales are falling from my eyes. Who is caught in night already considers the dawn, day, and a grey day, brightness, but what is it when the sun rises?

*Letters*
January 6, 1787

One must allow a transformation of oneself to occur. One cannot remain stuck to one's previous ideas any longer, and yet one cannot say in detail what the enlightenment consists of. ... I have only one existence; this time I have lived it fully, and still do. If I come out with body and soul, if my nature, my spirit, my happiness overcome this crisis, then I shall replace for you a thousand times what needs to be replaced. If I don't survive, I don't survive; without this, I was no good for anything any more.

*Letters*
January 17, 1787

From the Duke I received a letter, so mild, benevolent, sparing, supportive, and sincere that from this side my situation must appear to be most fortunate. And it will be, as soon as I think of myself alone; when I banish from my spirit that which I considered my duty for so long, and convince myself thoroughly that a human being should seize upon the good that occurs to him as fortunate booty, and should not concern himself left or right, and, even less, with the happiness or unhappiness of the whole. If one can be led to this state of mind, it is surely in Italy, especially in Rome. Here, where everyone lives for the moment, everyone wants, and must enrich himself, build a house for himself out of the ruins.

*Letters*
January 25, 1787

When Goethe abandoned the duties of Weimar to go to Rome, he proclaimed the "I-will" assertion of the lion, and for two years he pursued the activities he most loved. It was not a pleasure trip, as he often said, but a slow, hard-working, exhausting maturation. He went to be a part of the best the world had to offer. With great effort he sought to put into perspective his relations to the visual arts, his writing, his scientific investigations, and his friendships.

During those two years in Italy he gradually created a way of living that made him supremely happy. The heaviest price he paid for this discovery was undoubtedly the loss of the love and support of his friend Frau von Stein, who did not understand why he had to go to Rome to save his soul. That he was a happy man, despite the loss of this friend he loved, was reflected in his letters.

By the end of his stay in Rome, Goethe had finally come to see clearly what was most important for him. He was able to sort out the nature and extent of his creative gifts, which led to his realization that he was a poet, not a painter. In studying painting and natural science he had come to understand that there was one universal law valid for both art and science before which all that is arbitrary and imaginary collapses. Henceforth, for him to be happy, his hope was:

> Do not let [anything] come between me and the sun of sublime art and simple humanity. . . . I am too old for anything but truth.
>
> *Italian Journey*
> January 6, 1787

Goethe's self-understanding had reached the point that at last he could trust himself to return to Weimar without fear of being dominated again by Nietzsche's "thou-shalt" dragon. This new freedom for Goethe is reflected in his letters:

# The Art of Becoming Human

My existence has now acquired ballast that gives it the necessary weight; now I no longer fear the ghosts that so often played with me.

*Letters*
January 25, 1787

Rome is the only place in the world for an artist, and truly I am nothing other. I have made the acquaintance of happy people, who are so because they are whole; even the simplest, if he is whole, can be happy, and in his way complete. This is what I shall and must attain, and I can; at least I know where it lies and how it goes.

*Letters*
June 8, 1787

In going to Rome Goethe was following what Joseph Campbell called the "hero path": the departure from home on a quest, the fulfillment of an adventure, and the return home with new insights and a gentle heart. By the time he went back to Weimar the civil servant had become a human being, as undivided and undisturbed in himself as in the poem he wrote:

Nature gives everything richly and freely. She has neither pit nor rind; everything she is at once.

"Allerdings: Dem Physiker"

Most people do not go to Rome to find a more congenial way to live. Indeed, the search may take place anywhere in the world, even at home. Although no one is absolutely certain of what he or she is looking for, each one is confident that whatever it is, it will be recognized and able to be claimed. Anyone who finds what is his is suddenly at peace. The search is over. The proof is a sense of wholeness that clears the mind and permits a person to see. The root of the word *respect* (Latin: *respicio, re-specio*) is to see. To be able to see what is there—with respect—is the beginning of understanding.

In their forties most people experience a series of separations that take many different forms and unquestionably change their lives. Grown-up children are leaving to go to college or jobs away from home. Parents, remembering their own difficulties in this major separation, sympathize with their children's struggles. At the same time, the parents' attention is deflected from the past to often very acute present pangs of living in an empty nest. It is a glad-sad separation. Intellectually the fact that children leave home is acknowledged, but parents have grown so accustomed to them as a part of home life that they are dismayed when the time comes to let the children go.

> The daughter's daily request for freedom was answered by the daily promise of college. An unsteady bargain was struck. The mother gained time. She gathered herself together for parting. Cast her she would upon the water of life, but not now, not yet, and not upon any water. For the currents of that water, she determined, would never again return the daughter to that factory town.
>
> In 1928 the pledge of college was honorably met. The daughter left home for good and publicly the mother gave no sign of flinching.
>
> *The Blow upon the Heart*
> (Work in progress)

With the children gone, the underlying structure of the family—the marriage—is exposed to a closer look. Some marriages that seemed happy and secure with growing children, suddenly, unforeseeably, prove to be empty and pointless without them. Discontented, unhappy, distraught by what is, what was, and what might be, marriage partners frequently seek new alliances that chance so abundantly provides in today's permissive society.

> . . . Yet must Antony
> No way excuse his foils, when we do bear
> So great weight in his lightness. If he fill'd
> His vacancy with his voluptuousness,
> Full surfeits and the dryness of his bones
> Call on him for't. But to confound such time
> That drums him from his sport, and speaks as loud
> As his own state and ours, 'tis to be chid
> As we rate boys who, being mature in knowledge,
> Pawn their experience to their present pleasure,
> And so rebel to judgment.
>
> William Shakespeare
> *Antony and Cleopatra*
> Act 1, scene 4

Successful marriages bloom with or without children. Each partner may be deeply committed to an undertaking that he or she pursues with support from the other. Children of such a marriage are a living extension of a basic, continuing, workable union, a whole in which one plus one equals one.

Another kind of separation faces older adults and may occur at any time, but often happens by their late fifties. They lose their parents. In all too many instances the death of an elderly parent is not a sudden surprise, but follows a long, serious illness in which the grown children are intimately involved. The death of an aged parent is a sobering fact that thrusts the members of the family into a stark confrontation with reality. To their surprise, the older ones realize that now they are the senior members of the family.

How is death to be understood? Plato wept for Socrates—I weep, Socrates, not for you but for myself in having to lose such a friend—just as we weep for one we love who dies.

The recognition that sooner or later we shall follow them into the mystery of death can help us possibly more than any other experience in becoming a human being. It can change our way of living by making clear that now is the time to live with only the things that really matter to us.

How many people ever seriously consider their own death, once they have signed their last will and testament? Not many, I suspect. The subject is too morbid; the fear, postponed.

It may take a brush with the wings of death's angel to awaken a person to his own mortality, and to put his life into proper focus. In that instant, economics and politics drop away like lead sinkers, making it possible to float clear of such concerns. All the places in one's consciousness, formerly clogged with worldly cares, become filled with freedom and ease. The surrounding, tick-tock world is clearly *out there*; *in here* is an utterly private world in which one feels quiet, light, and unburdened. To people who have had this experience, such feelings are the most natural in the world. It is not frightening because they are not alone.

What is with them? Every person and thing in their entire life that they have truly loved, that has made them feel fully alive. Had they been poets, these are the people and things about which they would have sung their songs.

It may take a close call with death to show a person what he or she loves without qualification—and what that means exactly. All their lives they search outside themselves for what they lack, not realizing that it is not out there, beyond them, but in here, within them. The accumulated love of a lifetime is waiting silently to be claimed inside themselves.

In the moment that one finally grasps this reality—at whatever juncture in life and for whatever reason—the realization is decisive. Ever after, there is no need to hurry. One is not going anywhere; one has arrived.

Without such an experience, many adults may continue the search for the meaning of their own lives. Thoreau wrote of this search for something of one's own:

> I long ago lost a hound dog, a bay horse, and a turtle dove and am still on their trail. Many are the travellers I have spoken to concerning them. . . .

Henry David Thoreau
*Walden*

Most people in their fifties have dealt one way or another with the "thou-shalt" dragon and are as close to being a proclaiming "I-will" lion as they ever will be. But Nietzsche's further question is crucial: Have they also "created freedom for continued creating" in their lives?

Early adulthood may be thought of as the first beginning, but toward the end of middle adulthood the possibility of a new beginning becomes evident with the transfer of familiar responsibilities to others. It can be a transitional stage to the full freedom of late adulthood.

By the time people approach their sixtieth birthday, no matter what personal, lionlike successes or failures in life may be theirs—and as long as they are not completely ego-bound and hanging on to small ends—they know that there are greater powers than their own, somewhere out in the world, somewhere out in the universe. They see themselves as a tiny particle of the ever-expanding wholeness of nature.

# Middle Adulthood (Forty to Sixty Years)

\*   \*   \*

In the immensity and variety of human attainments throughout history, the three aristocrats, suggested by the nineteenth-century French poet Charles Baudelaire, are the poet, the soldier, and the priest. The decisive, civilizing voice of poets like Dante, Shakespeare, and Goethe; the magnitude and power of soldiers like Caesar, Alexander, and Napoleon; and the compassion and vision of priests like Christ, Buddha, and Mohammed have radiated far beyond the limits of their earthly existence. The passing centuries have not diminished their force. If we listen, they still speak to us. Their resonant words, brave endeavors, and sublime teachings can still stir our senses, awaken our strength and courage, and enhance our feeling of vitality.

We are unlikely to encounter personalities who approach the stature of these great human beings. And yet, everyone is endowed with some of the creative energy that these magnificent people had in such superabundance.

In ordinary living, occasionally, there is a glimpse, especially on the worldwide lens of television, of extraordinary acts of heroism that make everyone proud of being a human being. Then, as Emerson says, Jove nods to Jove above our heads.

On July 20, 1969, almost everyone who watched Neil Armstrong set his foot on the moon shared an enormous expansion of human horizons. Intellectually we know how small the earth is and how infinite the universe, but to see that smallness and that infinity so graphically demonstrated was awesome. This is as it should be. We need awe to keep our priorities straight.

By some extraordinary connection we are linked to these great forces. A flashing, private intimation is felt from time to time that may incline some to say with Dante,

115

# The Art of Becoming Human

Direct my mind to God in gratitude, who hath united us with the first star.

*The Divine Comedy, Paradiso*
Canto 2

# 6

# *Late Adulthood (Sixty Years On)*

*F*reud's prescription for a balanced life is work and love. The balance is fragile, being so much at the mercy of chance and the passage of time. For most people, half of Freud's prescription is automatically eliminated at age sixty-five. Social Security payments begin, working life ends, and retirement—not always of their own choosing—awaits. It is a major separation.

For those in good health on their sixty-fifth birthday, with all the energies of life, and managing not to fear illness while still well, retirement surely seems a waste of experience, knowledge, and talent. But it is usually only the self-employed who have the privilege of choice.

Some older people, of course, are glad to retire. Having worked hard or at least faithfully for forty years, they see retirement—supported by Social Security, pension plans, and IRAs—as a just reward. The pleasant thought of a secure financial future in which to do what one wishes, to go where one pleases, and to be at no one's beck and call, obscures the question of how, exactly, to spend leisure time. Retirement, at first, is equated with vacation, which, of course, it is not.

But there are many more employees who do not want the roots of work life disturbed, let alone cut. Confronted by the unsettling realization of their dependence upon the habit and routine of daily work, they feel threatened by its loss. Retirement looms as a menace. To imagine a future without a job, without the social contact of coworkers, without the interchange or even the clash of conflicting ideas, creates a state of great uncertainty.

Everyone's deepest yearning is for the order and connection of familiar things. Plans for tomorrow give today its shape and meaning. But now, the independence of retirement seems to some people a challenge, to others a source of dread.

By late adulthood, men and women are no strangers to separation, with its sequel of loss, dependence, initiative, and independence. But the separation of retirement is different. Now they are on their own, expected nowhere, needed by nobody, and responsible only to themselves. In an external, worldly sense, people are considered independent when they earn enough money to support their way of life—the more successful, the more independent.

At retirement, the word *independence* takes on a different meaning. It is *in-dependence*: a dependence upon their own inner resources. It means being responsible—responding to the potentially boundless inner life. It means freedom from the influence and external control of others. It means a shift from public recognition to private joy. The realization of the need to focus more intently upon one's inner life strikes home with force, often propelling people into entirely new, unforeseen directions.

During the Great Depression of the thirties, the Rockefeller Foundation funded a research project that looked forward to the possibility of a forty-hour work week. The question was posed:

How will people spend their leisure time? Research workers asked unemployed men and women: What would you do if you had a million dollars?

Today it might take seven million dollars to elicit the same responses. During the Depression, most people said that they would pay their debts, buy houses, clothes, cars, and maybe yachts, provide for their parents and close relatives, send their children to college, and then travel around the world. Underlying this phantasy was the deeper question: After you have done all that, what then? How do you want to spend your life? What attracts you? What makes you happy? Money buys choices but not happiness.

The celebratory aspect of retirement soon passes, leaving each adult with the problem of creating a different style of daily living. If a retiree does not know what he wants to do, or for some reason cannot do what he wants to do, he invents endless diversions to fight off the ennui that would otherwise afflict him. By avoidance, he spares himself a confrontation with the specific circumstances of his life that might drive him into despair.

A most poignant example is the life of the Duke of Windsor, who, in 1936, at the age of forty-two, abdicated as King Edward VIII of England to marry Wallis Simpson, a twice-divorced American woman. He gained "the woman I love" for the rest of his life—and he lived to his seventy-eighth year—but he lost his work, the occupation of king, the only job he knew. When he signed the Instruments of Abdication, he did not foresee that his brother, the new King George VI, would not find him some occupation, one that would make use of his great experience and popularity to benefit the British Empire. He never expected to be exiled from England. He certainly thought his wife would have the same royal rank as the wives of his younger brothers. Nor had he any reason to suppose that it would be prudent to settle future financial arrangements before his abdication. He spent a lifetime struggling—unsuccessfully—to correct these humiliating inequities. The Duke and Duchess of Windsor were compelled to live abroad as exiles—perpetual visitors and guests in the world throughout their long lifetimes. They were unwelcome in England, unwelcomed by the royal family, stripped of properties and monies. Despite the regal and affluent impression that they succeeded in maintaining, their life had a profoundly sad aspect to it.

In *King Lear,* Shakespeare gives us perhaps the most gripping and wrenching of all statements about the loss of kingly power. Like King Lear, the former King Edward VIII learned by swift and savage acts that with the loss of kingly power he became subject to inconceivable indignities, dishonors, and dishonesties: the chilling abandonment by every formerly deferential family member; the haughty disdain of once obsequious courtiers; and the unforgiving, unrelenting, shabby treatment by the British establishment, whose adulation of him as Prince of Wales had been so extravagant.

*Lear*    Why came not the slave back to me when I called him?

*Knight*  Sir, he answered me in roundest manner, he would not.

*Lear*    He would not!

*Knight*  My lord, I know not what the matter is; but to my judgment, your highness is not entertained with that ceremonious affection as you were wont. There's a great abatement of kindness appears as well in the general dependents as in the Duke also and your daughter.

*Lear*    Ha! sayest thou so?

*Knight*  I beseech you, pardon me, my lord, if I be mistaken; for my duty cannot be silent when I think your highness wronged.

*Lear*    Thou but remember'st me of mine own conception. I

|      | have perceived a most faint neglect of late, which I have rather blamed as mine own jealous curiosity than as a very pretense and purpose of unkindness. I will look further into it. . . . |
|------|------|
| *Lear* | Dost thou call me fool, boy? |
| *Fool* | All thy other titles thou has given away; that thou was born with. |

William Shakespeare
*King Lear*
Act 1, scene 4

There is a power of office that belongs to every occupation. It may not be the power of a king, but in virtually every sphere of work there is status and recognition connected with a job. At retirement the specific power and authority of an office is gone. That power may have been ours for so many years that we do not know who we are without its privileges. It has become a part of our identity, and with its loss we feel disenfranchised. This unexpected and surprising aspect of retirement makes a redefinition of ourselves imperative. As long as we are recognized and remembered by former associates, the old courtesies continue, but when new, younger people fill the ranks, we are ignored. Who are we without our identifying attributes?

Only a grandchild in earliest childhood will listen attentively to where we have been and what we have done and believe every word. A small child is a true believer, and there is no more devoted audience. So, it happens that in the late afternoon of adult life, enthusiastic welcome is offered by one at the beginning of life. Both old and young persons, free of external demands, have unhurried time for each other. Each is engrossed in the adventure of his own life: a grandparent tells his story; a small child reacts to the everchanging, present moment, which is so fair.

# The Art of Becoming Human

Today more and more individuals in late adulthood are destined to experience the new, unexplored, extended years of old, old age. For them, Nietzsche, in a grand, circular sweep of thought, envisions another potential transformation:

> But tell me, my brethren, why hath the preying lion still to become a child? Innocence is the child, and forgetfulness, a new beginning, a game, a self-rolling wheel, a first movement, a holy Yea. Aye, for the game of creating, my brethren, there is needed a holy Yea unto life: its own will, willeth now the spirit; his own world winneth the world's outcast. Three metamorphoses of the spirit have I designated to you: how the spirit became a camel, the camel a lion, and the lion at last a child.
>
> Friedrich Nietzsche
> *Thus Spake Zarathustra*

If older men and women have the courage to accept the continuing challenge of this freedom, to say a holy Yea unto life, to escape the engulfment of the things of time, to create new values, and to use their leisure to do something of absorbing interest, they can join "the game of creating." There is no authority, no power, no status associated with it. They do it as children do it, for sheer pleasure and joy.

A love of life that is discounted in the hectic adult, workaday world may be rediscovered through children. How is this accomplished? How do you relate to an infant, for instance? Infants seem to look alike unless details are examined. The first step is to be quiet enough to see the infant without words or thought, just as he is. An infant is not self-conscious, so that it does not embarrass him if you look straight at him. In fact, that is how the infant looks at you. Nothing else is necessary. Slow down to the infant's pace, that is all.

To a preoccupied, busy adult, at first sight, it seems as if the infant has no pace, is even static, but this is not true. The infant's movements are slow, deliberate, observable, and if you quiet down to his rhythm, you will see the infant clearly: a small, physically complete, utterly unselfconscious human being, who is his own unique self and no one else. And in startling contrast to the complete helplessness of the infant's body is the sovereignty of his objective gaze.

At birth, the infant has no outer, protective, social covering composed of knowledge, experience, memory, and self-consciousness. The unadulterated essence of an infant's inner life is exposed to view if anyone cares to look. To see the infant in this manner, forget what you know; just look and delight in what you see.

It is not easy to slow down enough to look, even if it is to see more clearly. Joseph Campbell remarked that Odysseus, returning home from the bloody, rough days of the Trojan War, needed ten disastrous years of wandering to slow down enough to return to Ithaca—sufficiently humbled—to become a considerate husband to Penelope and a gentle father to Telemachus.

Retirement from the stresses and strains of public life enables many older adults to relearn how to be simple, direct, and without guile. Children accept people only on these terms, if anything real is to happen between them. When time is spent with a child in this manner, the experience is memorable. A child does not need to share his private life with anyone in order to grow up, but if, by chance, an adult is able to participate—without intrusion or disturbance—in the pleasure of the child's absorption in the present moment, it is heaven.

The opportunity to experience this wonderful relationship with a child is not strictly limited to grandchildren. It can happen between any child and any adult who are in tune with each other.

If a person has never learned how to relate to a child, how is it possible to relate to one's own creative self? How can one join Nietzsche's "game of creating" if its rules and purpose are unknown? How can one know its joyfulness? Each person has to ask himself if he is really serious, respectful, and reverent about creating.

If in a long lifetime people learn that getting and spending is not enough to satisfy them, there is still time to learn other ways of living that have more meaning. If the adventure of becoming a human being has always been postponed, there is still time to set forth. Even Scrooge, in Dickens's *Christmas Carol,* was able to accomplish it.

When an individual pays attention to something of enormous interest to him—finding out all about it, and giving his heart to it—new ideas vivid with novelty and unexpected possibilities may miraculously occur to him. The task he sets himself is one he wants to do, not one he has to do. The engagement of natural talent and ability, his *daimon,* with the work at hand is so purely voluntary—thus, perfectly direct, uncomplicated, and simple— that what he creates transmits all of his unimpeded, fresh vitality. This process, without conscious intention, is likely to have a harmonious rhythm of its own that surprises and delights its creator. As Alfred North Whitehead would say, it becomes his romance.

When retired people explore these new dimensions, they often find that their gifts vary in depth and richness. A poet sings the soaring songs in his soul, perhaps awakening a slumbering echo in another. An organizer may find a community project that needs a volunteer. A craftsman uses his tools to translate a theoretical concept into a tangible form. Cooks cook. Gardeners garden.

There is no end to the possible uses of leisure time. In earlier years these activities were often hobbies. But now, with more leisure, an unused channel for new creating may be opened—if they are serious about it. A vision of something they love to do may lead them to new "work" that gives a fresh beginning to each day.

It becomes easier to understand the friends of their youth who refused the burdens of the camel and the pride of the lion in order to give expression to the force of their own inner vision. In late adulthood they may look back at those youthful adventurers with great sympathy, realizing, at last, how strong they were to go against the tide of conformity. It is, perhaps, clearer now what Thoreau meant about his lost hound dog, bay horse, and turtle dove. They may even join those who seemed as anxious to recover them, as if they had lost them themselves.

In addition to these new preoccupations there remains a multitude of practical decisions to be made about the future. Retirement plans require careful consideration in order to reduce the risks of chance. Nobody can afford to make too many flagrant mistakes about time or money in late adulthood.

One of the first decisions may be to move to a warm climate. The enjoyment of life has much to do with the weather, and so retired people move, despite a preference for the old and familiar. Or they may move from the city to the country, or to a place nearer to their children, or to any number of places for any number of personal reasons. This transplantation to a new environment, a new landscape, a new house, new neighbors, new doctors, dentists, merchants, and service people of every variety consumes time and energy, and may sweep them into their seventies before they feel settled and in place again.

No one mentions the amount of paperwork that is involved in retirement. Workers pay for Social Security, IRAs, and the like, for so many years that it comes almost as a shock when payments to them begin. Retirees now find their private lives inundated with endless business forms, government directives, and insurance policies. Now they are at their desks working for themselves. This essential desk work is the business and banking aspect of their lives that never ends so long as there are bills to be paid. Eventually, the fortunate ones bring order into their financial affairs, which is important, since money permits choice and order saves time.

The opportunity to travel more widely and with more leisure may spur wanderlust and curiosity. The entire world opens up. Tourists go on tours to be spared the bother of planning their trips, especially to foreign lands where they have never been and whose language they do not speak. More experienced travelers find that part of their satisfaction lies in planning their trips. They go to new places as if by appointment. The more they know about the countries they visit, the more pleasure they derive from the trip, and they make what they see their own.

There is travel of a different kind, as Goethe shows in his letters from Italy. This travel is intimate, driven by an overwhelming emotional need. If someone has had a lifelong love affair with a country—studying, reading, listening to others talk about it—until finally an opportunity comes to visit, no one could possibly plan the trip for that lover. He or she knows precisely where to go, what to see, and in what order and for how long. That trip is a pilgrimage and it will be etched forever in that pilgrim's heart. There are no words to describe the experience nor is there need to do so. It is a private, secret joy best referred to by indirection.

The joy of love for a place, a person, or a thing is singularly and essentially private, but its radiance is reflected, attracting public attention that often stimulates envy. In *The Rape of Lucrece*, Shakespeare shows us how poor Collatine paid dearly for speaking about what was dearest to him, his wife.

> When Collatine unwisely did not let
> To praise the clear unmatched red and white

Which triumph'd in that sky of his delight
Where mortal stars, as bright as heaven's beauties,
With pure aspects did him peculiar duties.

For he, the night before, in Tarquin's tent,
Unlocked the treasure of his happy state;
What priceless wealth the heavens had him lent
In the possession of his beauteous mate;
Reckoning his fortune at such high-proud rate,
That kings might be espoused to more fame,
But king nor peer to such a peerless dame.

O happiness enjoy'd but of a few!
And, if possess'd, as soon decay'd and done
As is the morning's silver-melting dew
Against the golden splendour of the sun;
An expir'd date, cancelled ere well begun:
Honour and beauty, in the owner's arms,
Are weakly fortress'd from a world of harms.

Beauty itself doth of itself persuade
The eyes of men without an orator;
What needeth then apology be made
To set forth that which is so singular?
Or why is Collatine the publisher
Of that rich jewel he should keep unknown
From thievish ears, because it is his own?

It is best to guard the source of private joy from thievish ears.
But even if happiness is silently contained within ourselves, still
it will overflow and transform everything we do and say, so that
indirectly our love is shared by all. It is enough for the world to
love the lover—not his love.

The day comes, finally, when a person stays home and looks
around to see where he is, what he is doing, and how he feels

about his life. If he is fortunate enough to remain in good health in his seventies, he is aware that this is the time to pull the threads together and to receive his life.

As physical energies lessen, there is more time and quiet in which to think. Staring straight at him is the admonition at the sanctuary of Apollo in Delphi: Know thyself. What does this actually mean? If the question is frightening—or boring—he immediately flies into an activity with a specific date and hour. A busy, ceaselessly occupied mind keeps him from looking at the ice-cold truth of his life. The habit of escape into busyness reasserts itself. But if he stays the course and really wants to say a holy Yea to life, there are teachers and guides to help.

How can he look at himself objectively? His gaze is usually focused on the world outside. How can he turn around to look with intense scrutiny at the world inside himself, a process leading hopefully to insight? To remember and to know does not help. The past is finished and done with. Instead, he must listen to the thoughts that are chattering in his head, and feel the feelings that are clamoring for attention right now.

He becomes acutely aware of how necessary it is to contain these thoughts and feelings privately within himself so that he can look at them quietly and gently, excluding nothing, without explanation, without purpose, and especially without criticism. What is crucial is to watch the flow and ebb of feelings and thoughts without complaint, excuse, or disdain.

Why? Because these thoughts and feelings are precisely who he is at that instant. Human thoughts and feelings are the raw materials of who a person is. Responses to relationships with people, ideas, things, and ourselves stir thoughts and feelings into life.

What separates us from each other is what we choose to do with our thoughts and feelings. Goethe's play *Torquato Tasso,* based on the early life of this famous sixteenth-century Italian poet at the court of Ferrara, describes the impetuous outburst of intemperate feelings that precipitates Tasso's tragic undoing as a court poet. He believed that his poetry made him the equal of the nobility, but he found out that he was mistaken. At the urging of the Princess, whom he loves, Torquato Tasso offers his friendship to Antonio, the Secretary of State of the Court of Ferrara, and trusted adviser to the Princess's brother, Alfonso, the Duke of Ferrara; Antonio rebuffs him.

| | |
|---|---|
| *Antonio* | You prove me right yourself in spurning you! And so the over-hasty boy would get By force the grown man's confidence and friendship? Ill-bred as you are, do you think you're so good? |
| *Tasso* | Far rather what you choose to term ill-bred Than what I could not help but term ignoble. |
| *Antonio* | You still are young enough that proper training Can teach you something of a better way. |
| *Tasso* | Not young enough to bow in front of idols; To brave defiance with defiance, old enough. |
| *Antonio* | Where lip and lyre decide the contest You do come off the hero and the victor. |
| *Tasso* | It would be rash to boast about my fists; They have done nothing, but I trust in them. |
| *Antonio* | You reckon on forbearance, which has only Spoiled you too much in arrogant good fortune. |
| *Tasso* | That I am grown to manhood, I now feel. You are the last with whom I should have liked To try the hazard of a pass with weapons, But you rake fire on top of fire until My inmost marrow scorches and the painful Lust for revenge seethes foaming in my breast. |

# The Art of Becoming Human

|          | So if you are the man you boast of, face me. |
|----------|----------------------------------------------|
| *Antonio* | You know as little who, as where, you are. |
| *Tasso* | No sanctuary bids us bear abuse. |
|         | You blaspheme and desecrate this place, |
|         | Not I, who offered you my confidence, |
|         | Respect, and love, the finest offerings. |
|         | Your spirit has defiled this paradise |
|         | And your words now defile this stainless room, |
|         | Not my heart's surge of passion which now rages |
|         | At suffering the slightest spot of soilure. |
| *Antonio* | What lofty spirit in that pent-up bosom! |
| *Tasso* | Here is still room to give that bosom vent. |
| *Antonio* | The rabble also vent their hearts with words. |
| *Tasso* | If you're a nobleman as I am, show it. |
| *Antonio* | Such am I, but I know, too, where I am. |
| *Tasso* | Come down then where our weapons may avail. |
| *Antonio* | You should not challenge, and I will not come. |
| *Tasso* | Such obstacles are welcome to a coward. |
| *Antonio* | The coward threatens only where he is safe. |
| *Tasso* | With joy I can dispense with that protection. |
| *Antonio* | You compromise yourself, this place you cannot. |
| *Tasso* | The place forgive me for enduring this. |

(He draws his sword.)

Draw or come after, if I am not to
Despise you, as I hate you, evermore.

(Enter Alfonso.)

| *Alfonso* | In what contention do I chance upon you? |
| *Antonio* | You find me standing calmly, O my Prince, |
|         | Before a man whom rage has seized upon. |
| *Tasso* | Ah, I adore you as a deity, for |
|         | Restraining me with just one glance of warning. |
| *Alfonso* | Recount, Antonio, Tasso, and inform me |
|         | How did dissension get into my house? |
|         | How did it seize upon you, carrying off |

In a frenzy sane men from the path of proper
Behavior and laws? I am astonished!

The alternative to giving our passions free rein is restraining
them, containing them, even transmuting their force to peaceful
ends. The choice is ours to make, however much we may deny it!

In contrast to Tasso's intemperate rage, Shakespeare portrays
noblesse oblige—sovereignty—on the highest level in Antony's
treatment of Enobarbus in *Antony and Cleopatra*. (Enobarbus,
the trusted friend and companion of Antony, turned traitor and
joined Caesar Octavian when Antony was defeated at Actium.
Nonetheless, Antony not only returned all of Enobarbus's personal possessions, but sent additional treasure after him.)

*Enobarbus*  I have done ill,
            Of which I do accuse myself so sorely
            That I will joy no more.
                    (Enter a Soldier of Caesar's . . .)
*Soldier*  Enobarbus, Antony
            Hath after thee sent all thy treasure,
            With his bounty overplus. The messenger
            Came on my guard, and at my tent is now
            Unloading of his mules.
*Enobarbus*  I give it you.
*Soldier*  Mock not, Enobarbus,
            I tell you true: . . .
            Your emperor continues still a Jove.
                  (Soldier exits.)
*Enobarbus*  I am alone the villain of the earth,
            And feel I am so most. O Antony,
            Thou mine of bounty, how wouldst thou
            Have paid my better service, when my
            Turpitude thou dost so crown with gold!

This blows my heart: If swift thought
Break it not, a swifter mean shall
Outstrike thought; but thought will do't,
I feel. I fight against thee! No: I
Will go seek some ditch, wherein to die;
The foul'st best fits my latter part
Of life. . . .

*Enobarbus* Throw my heart against the flint and
Hardness of my fault. . . . O Antony,
Nobler than my revolt is infamous,
Forgive me in thine own particular,
But let the world rank me in register,
A master leaver and a fugitive.
O Antony! O Antony!
(Dies.)

Act 4, scenes 5 and 7

People differ in their ability to contain negative thoughts and feelings. They differ, too, in what they can and cannot control. Some people can control feelings of physical pain, but may have less control, as Kierkegaard has pointed out, if they lose five dollars or a wife.

Most thoughtful people are aware of the role that feeling and thought play in relationships. With closer examination of that role, what may become clearer is the possibility of coping with interpersonal problems in an entirely different way, resulting in happier relationships.

When we consider the discrepancy between what we want and what we get—the cause of intensely negative feelings—that discrepancy is breathtaking. What we want from others is according to us, and what we get from others is according to them—and we both may be right.

If a well-entrenched "according to me" idea is on a collision course with a strongly held "according to you" opinion, progress can begin only when we acknowledge the right of each to his or her own point of view.

Slowly, painfully, we begin to realize that, unbeknownst to others, we project our needs and wishes onto them—needs and wishes that not only have nothing to do with them, but often are of such a completely unacceptable nature that it is impossible for our expectations to be met. Suddenly, our righteous indignation begins to look extremely inappropriate, and even slightly ridiculous, and our anger disappears into thin air.

Of course, wishes and expectations may still remain, but we do not have to hurt ourselves and others by foisting them onto people unable to meet them. It is wiser to wonder where our needs and wishes come from, and, if they remain important, to do something about them ourselves.

Goethe told Eckermann long ago that it was a great folly to hope that other men would harmonize with us, and that it was best to regard each man or woman as an independent individual, and thus come to know the flexibility necessary for the conduct of life among so many different characters.

When we look at our thoughts rather than think them, how judgmental are they? Do we criticize others in our minds, even though we keep strict control of our tongues? Are we surprised at the amount of space that judgment and condemnation occupy in our thoughts? How much time and energy do we waste in explanation and justification? Why do we bother? Why not let it be? What are we trying to prove? And why do we hurt ourselves by comparing? Is it not enough to see it? And how much time do we waste over choices that may never be ours to make?

We begin to realize that the composition of our thoughts and feelings is no different from those of our neighbors—it is the human condition. This revelation is profound and extremely humbling. We are not unique, after all.

A great new freedom becomes ours when we accept the differences of others, differences that are an endlessly fascinating source of inspiration to all great artists. Goethe shows us how Shakespeare used this boundless raw material of human thoughts and feelings in his plays, works that tell us so much about human beings that it seems as if nothing is left to be said.

> The highest to which man can attain is the consciousness of his own ideas and thoughts, the recognition of himself which gives him the means of completely recognizing the hearts of others. Now there are people who are born with a natural predisposition for this and who develop it through experience for practical purposes. Thence comes the capacity to profit from the world and its affairs. . . .
>
> With this predisposition also the poet is born, only that he develops it not for immediate earthly purposes. If, now, we call Shakespeare one of the greatest poets, we immediately concede that no one easily understood the world as he, that no one has expressed his inner vision so well, transporting the reader to a consciousness of the world on a higher level. The world becomes totally transparent to us; we find ourselves suddenly the intimates of virtue and vice, of greatness and pettiness, of nobility and degradation, and all of this, indeed, even more, through the simplest means. But if we ask about these means, it seems as though he works for our eyes; but we are misled. Shakespeare's works are not for the eyes of the body. . . .
>
> Shakespeare speaks consistently to our inner sense; through it, the world of images of the imagination is activated, . . . it is here that the reason lies for the illusion that everything is taking place before our eyes. But if we consider Shakespeare's works carefully, they contain much less action per-

ceptible through the senses than words for the spirit. . . . According to the description of the characters we do create certain images, but we discover through a succession of words and speeches what occurs within their hearts, and here all participants seem to have agreed among themselves not to leave us in the dark, or in doubt about anything . . . everything that hides in the heart of men in moments of awesome occurrences is expressed; what a soul fearfully shuts in and conceals is brought to light freely and fluidly; we experience the touch of life and do not know how. Shakespeare allies himself with the spirit of the world. He pervades the world as does the spirit. Nothing is hidden to either. But while it is the world-spirit's business to preserve secrets before, and indeed often after, the deed, it is the idea of the poet to blabber the secret, and to make us intimates before, or indeed, in the act. . . . The vice-ridden man of power, the well-intentioned man of limited scope, the man who is passionately carried away, the one who contemplates quietly, all carry their hearts in their hands, often against all plausibility; every one speaks much and gladly. . . . The secret must come out, even if the stones reveal it.

Johann Wolfgang von Goethe
"Shakespeare and No End"

No one, possibly, has made a stronger statement than this about the fact that a consciousness of one's own thoughts and feelings is the highest to which man can attain. We are living people, not characters in a Shakespearean play, but the thoughts and feelings of his characters are often no different from our own. The revelation of his plays lies in observing what happens when nothing is disguised, nothing withheld, and nothing is going to waste. All barriers of time and space—even of animate and inanimate things—vanish. We are mad· ·o relate to everyone and everything by means of the thoughts, perceptions, and feelings that are given to human beings. While outer circumstances and costumes differ, Shakespeare dramatizes the unchanging aspects of the human heart and mind.

Human beings can contain negative thinking—if they so choose—and, looking at it without action, may even see it dissipate under an impartial, objective gaze. The expression of positive feelings, if not possessive, always is a pleasure.

With containment of thoughts and feelings, listening changes. The old way of listening to literal content is usually judgmental; the new listening is to feelings and thinking—ours and theirs. Human behavior may consciously or unconsciously be in startling contradiction to speech. But to be able to look and listen with free-floating attention, without the intrusion of words, makes another person more transparent and understandable. We begin to appreciate what it means to love our neighbor as ourselves. This insight may lead to a deeply penetrating, compassionate understanding and concern for another human being. Noblesse oblige is firmly rooted in this fertile soil.

Looking and listening with free-floating attention permits the inner radiance of another to shine through. In the great wealth of the world's literature, a peerless description of such a change in the way of looking and listening to others appears in *War and Peace.*

> Pierre was hardly changed in his external habits. In appearance he was just the same as before. He was, as he had always been, absent-minded, and seemed preoccupied with something of his own, something apart from what was before his eyes. The difference was that in the old days, when he was unconscious of what was before his eyes, or what was being said to him, he would seem with painfully knitted brows to be striving unsuccessfully to discern something far away from him. . . .

But now with a faint, apparently ironical smile, he gazed at what was before him, or listened to what was said, though he was obviously seeing and hearing something quite different. In the old days he had seemed a good-hearted man, but unhappy. And so people had unconsciously held a little aloof from him. Now a smile of joy in life was continually playing about his mouth, and his eyes were bright with sympathy for others, and the question: Were they all as happy as he? And people felt at ease in his presence.

In the old days he had talked a great deal, and had got hot when he talked, and he had listened very little. Now he was rarely carried away in conversation, and knew how to listen, so that people were very ready to tell him the inmost secret of their hearts.

The princess who had never liked Pierre, and had cherished a particularly hostile feeling towards him, but after the old count's death she had felt herself under obligation to him, had come to Orel with the intention of proving to him that in spite of his ingratitude she felt it her duty to nurse him, but after a short time she felt, to her own surprise and annoyance, that she was growing fond of him. Pierre did nothing to try to win his cousin's favor; he simply looked at her with curiosity. In the old days she had felt that there was mockery and indifference in his eyes, and she had shrunk into herself before him, as she did before other people, and had shown him only her aggressive side. Now she felt, on the contrary, as though he were delving into the most secret recesses of her life. It was at first mistrustfully, and then with gratitude, that she let him see now the latent good side of her character.

The most artful person could not have stolen into the princess's confidence more cunningly, by arousing her recollections of the best time of her youth, and showing sympathy with them. And yet all Pierre's artfulness consisted in seeking to please himself by drawing out human qualities in the bitter, hard, and, in her own way, proud princess. . . .

# The Art of Becoming Human

The doctor, who was attending Pierre, and came to see him every day, though he thought it his duty as a doctor to pose as a man every minute of whose time is of value for suffering humanity, used to sit on with him for hours together, repeating his favorite anecdotes and observations on the peculiarities of patients in general, and of ladies in particular.

"Yes, it's a pleasure to talk to a man like that; it's not what we are used to in the provinces," he would say.

In Orel there happened to be several French prisoners, and the doctor brought one of them, a young Italian officer, to see Pierre. This officer became a frequent visitor, and the princess used to laugh at the tender feelings the Italian expressed for Pierre.

It was obvious that the Italian was never happy but when he could see Pierre, and talk to him, and tell him all about his own past, his homelife, and his love, and pour out his indignation against the French, and especially against Napoleon.

"If all Russians are the least bit like you," he used to say to Pierre, "it is sacrilege to make war on people like yours. You who have suffered so much at the hands of the French have not even a grudge against them."

And Pierre had won the Italian's passionate devotion simply by drawing out what was best in his soul and admiring it.

Leo Tolstoy
*War and Peace*

Tolstoy's description of Pierre's way of listening seems so remarkably simple. It is, if unruly passions have been tamed, and if a man or woman has been so extraordinarily fortunate as to become free—at least, to some extent—from the fear that to cease to assert himself would be to cease to exist.

Listening is an art, and, perhaps, no one listens well enough. In fact, it is very seductive to be listened to, and everyone is acutely aware of it when it happens. Thinking is a private occupation, and no matter how people may speculate, no one knows your exact thoughts for sure, unless you tell them. When someone listens without interruption to what you say, there is an increasing temptation to let one thought spark off another by association. Then even the speaker may be surprised and caught off guard by his own unexpected pronouncements. It is almost as if the speaker did not know his or her own thoughts until they were said. And the listener is acutely aware that the truth is being spoken.

The evenly hovering attention of the listener has much the same quality as the free associations of the speaker. Complete attention is shared by both. Each has suspended critical judgment. The listener is nonintrusive, meticulously avoiding speculation or reflection, simply letting everything come to him without selection or preference.

It demands an enormous tolerance to listen to someone else's thoughts, feelings, and especially repetitions without becoming impatient or even overwhelmed. For these reasons most people cannot listen for long without discomfort and increasing vexation that often makes them abruptly interrupt the speaker.

But there comes a time when speaking and listening no longer matter. Death is the last great adventure—the last separation. Its earthly aspect is well known, as one by one the people we love disappear into its unknown dimensions. We know the anguish of separation from them, the continuing sense of their presence, and, even after half a lifetime, the glow of their memory.

Those unfortunate ones whose fate it is to die in mind before dying in body are surrounded, unaware, by the unspeakable grief of those who love them, who have to stand by helplessly. It is so much harder for them.

## The Art of Becoming Human

Her eyes are fled
Into the deep dark cabins of her head:
Where they resign their office and their light
To the disposing of her troubled brain;
Who bids them still consort with ugly night,
And never wound the heart with looks again.

William Shakespeare
"Venus and Adonis"

But what of the experience of death itself—one's own future adventure? It begs the question to say that it is a nothingness. One difference is that loss of consciousness, unlike sleep, is irreversible. Order and connection are such basic, comforting facts in life, perhaps in death there is an order and connection of a different sort. A growing number of people who have suffered near-death experiences speak of an out-of-body consciousness that is filled with light and peace and beauty.

When, in life, love begins to fill the space between human beings, who have learned to transmute their anger to peaceful ends, some would speculate that, in death, they will find an infinite love that fills the space between them and infinity.

O Light eternal, who only in thyself abidest, only thyself dost understand, and to thyself, self-understood, self-understanding, turnest love and smiling.

Dante Alighieri
*The Divine Comedy, Paradiso*
Canto 33

In dying, one faces the final separation from an experience of the known of here—and moves toward an idea of the unknown of there. Goethe's Faust, turning for his last look at the world,

140

said, "Then dare I hail the moment fleeing: Ah, still delay, thou art so fair." Separation from the beauty of the earth does not strip us of the closeness of our very own inner life. We do not slip from the now of here to the now of there empty-handed. We take our love with us.

The pattern of love and separation at every stage of human development is self-evident, but does this pattern have a deeper meaning? It seems to be so. The theme of private life is played out in a parallel fashion in early childhood and early adulthood. Public life, the next theme, belongs to middle childhood and middle adulthood. Late childhood tries to unite in an unsteady and awkward way the private and public aspects of life. Late adulthood has the possibility and privilege in a broader, more sovereign way of uniting the inner mind with the outer universe to achieve an understanding of wholeness in which there is love and no separation.

# Notes to the Quotations

## Introduction

"I long ago lost a hound . . ." Henry David Thoreau, *Walden*, in *The Works of Henry David Thoreau* (New York: Thomas Y. Crowell Co., 1940), p. 20.

"We have only to follow the thread . . ." Joseph Campbell, *The Hero With a Thousand Faces* (New York: Meridian Books, 1958), p. 25.

## Chapter 1

"Even as the sun and planets stood to salute one another . . ." Johann Wolfgang von Goethe, "First, Last Words, Orphic: Destiny," *Selected Verse*, D. Luke, ed. (New York: Penguin, 1981), p. 302.

"Our birth is but a sleep and a forgetting . . ." William Wordsworth, "Ode: Intimations of Immortality from Recollections of Early Childhood," *The College Book of Verse*, Robert M. Gay, ed. (Boston: Houghton Mifflin, 1927), p. 328.

# The Art of Becoming Human

"How should I guard my soul so that it be/Not touched by thine? . . ." Rainer Maria Rilke, "The Song of Love," *An Anthology of World Poetry*, Mark Van Doren, ed. (New York: Harcourt, Brace, 1928), p. 937.

"We are told nothing of conception . . ." Carson McCullers, "Hymen, O Hymen," *The Mortgaged Heart,* Margarita G. Smith, ed. (Boston: Houghton Mifflin, 1971), p. 289.

"My sole consolation when I went upstairs for the night . . ." Marcel Proust, *Swann's Way*, C. K. Scott Moncrieff, trans. (New York: Modern Library, 1928), p. 18.

"I faint! O Iras! . . ." William Shakespeare, *Antony and Cleopatra*, Peter G. Phialas, ed., *The Yale Shakespeare* (New Haven, Conn.: Yale University Press, 1955), act 2, scene 5, line 112.

"Whoever weeps somewhere out in the world . . ." Rainer Maria Rilke, "Silent Hour," Jesse Lemont, trans., *Anthology of World Poetry,* p. 938.

"Frail the white rose . . ." James Joyce, "A Flower Given to My Daughter," *The Portable James Joyce* (New York: Viking, 1961), p. 650.

"My impression as a child was always that my father was not very much older than we were. . . ." Virginia Woolf, "Impressions of Sir Leslie Stephen," *The Essays of Virginia Woolf*, vol. 1, Andrew McNeillie, ed. (New York: Harvest/HBJ, 1986), p. 127.

"Unfortunately, too, the principle of discipline that young persons should be early deprived of all fear . . ." Johann Wolfgang von Goethe, *The Autobiography of Goethe: Truth and Poetry*, vol. 1, John Oxenford, trans. (London: George Bell and Sons, 1881), p. 4.

"Who is able to speak worthily of the fullness of childhood. . . ." Goethe, *Autobiography of Goethe*, p. 54.

## Chapter 2

"You may accumulate a vast amount of knowledge . . ." Arthur Schopenhauer, "On Thinking for Yourself," *Essays and Aphorisms*, R. J. Hollingdale, trans. (New York: Viking Penguin, 1986), pp. 89–91.

"Children . . . have an instinct resembling that possessed by rats and mice . . ." Johann Wolfgang von Goethe, *Wilhelm Meister's Apprenticeship*, R. Dillon Boylan, trans. (London: George Bell & Sons, 1883), p. 11.

"Now you can apply yourself voluntarily to reading and writing . . ." Schopenhauer, *Essays and Aphorisms*, p. 89.

"As the children of the cultivated classes grow up . . ." Goethe, *Autobiography of Goethe*, p. 51.

"Man's attitude toward authority . . . is a perpetual seesaw. . . ." Johann Wolfgang von Goethe, "On the Theory of Color," *Goethe: Wisdom and Experience*, H. J. Weigand, trans. and ed. (New York: Frederick Ungar Publishing Co., 1964), p. 186.

"Do not think the youth has no force because he cannot speak to you and me. . . ." Ralph Waldo Emerson, *Emerson's Essays* (New York: Thos. Nelson & Sons, no date), pp. 41–42.

"Richest in almost incomprehensible experience, however, were the birthdays. . . ." Rainer Maria Rilke, *The Notebooks of Malte Laurids Brigge*, M. D. Herter Norton, trans. (W. W. Norton, 1949), pp. 128–29.

"When children play they can make something out of anything. . . ." Johann Wolfgang von Goethe, *Wilhelm Meister's Apprenticeship*, Eric A. Blackall, trans. (New York: Suhrkamp Publishers, 1989), p. 21.

" 'Look,' John Henry said, and he was staring out the window. . . ." Carson McCullers, *The Member of the Wedding* (Boston: Houghton Mifflin, 1946), pp. 10–11.

## Chapter 3

"And sure enough, it comes." Johann Wolfgang von Goethe, "First and Last Words, Orphic: Love," *Selected Verse,* p. 303.

"Thus, at certain epochs, children part from parents, servants from masters, protégés from their patrons. . . ." Goethe, *Autobiography of Goethe,* p. 203.

"Bid adieu, adieu, adieu/Bid adieu to girlish days . . ." James Joyce, "Chamber Music," *Portable James Joyce,* p. 634.

"Being your slave what should I do but tend/Upon the hours and times of your desire? . . ." William Shakespeare, *Sonnets* (New York: E. P. Dutton, 1919), LVII.

"It is hard to explain scientifically, Son, he said. . . ." Carson Mc-Cullers, "A Tree · A Rock · A Cloud," *Collected Short Stories* (Boston: Houghton Mifflin, 1955), p. 103.

"First of all, love is a joint experience between two persons . . ." Carson McCullers, "The Ballad of the Sad Café, *Collected Short Stories* (Boston: Houghton Mifflin, 1955), p. 18.

"*Romeo.* Thou chid'st me often for loving Rosaline. *Friar.* For doting, not for loving, pupil mine. . . ." William Shakespeare, *Romeo and Juliet, The Yale Shakespeare,* act 2, scene 2, lines 77–90.

"*Antony.* I have offended reputation/A most unnoble swerving. . . ." Shakespeare, *Antony and Cleopatra,* act 3, scene 9, lines 49–70.

"If life is a kind of activity . . ." Marsilio Ficino, *The Letters of Marsilio Ficino* (London: Shepheard-Walwyn, 1978), pp. 188–89.

"Oh most wonderful intelligence of the heavenly architect! . . ." Marsilio Ficino, *Letters,* pp. 190–91.

"Do you know the land where the lemon tree blossoms? . . ." Johann Wolfgang von Goethe, "The Minstrel," *Selected Verse,* pp. 85–86.

"I worked with the intention of consulting you. . . ." Johann Wolfgang von Goethe, letter to J. G. Herder, *Goethe's World*, Berthold Biermann, ed. (New York: New Directions, 1949), p. 58.

"When the soul of man is born in this country . . ." James Joyce, *A Portrait of the Artist as a Young Man, Portable James Joyce,* p. 468.

"Away! Away! The spell of arms and voices . . ." James Joyce, *A Portrait of the Artist as a Young Man, Portable James Joyce,* p. 525.

## Chapter 4

"Every bird has its decoy . . ." Goethe, *Autobiography of Goethe,* p. 135.

"I had lost that unconscious happiness of wandering. . . ." Goethe, *Autobiography of Goethe,* pp. 185–86.

"*Prince.* And princes all, I beseech you . . ." William Shakespeare, *King Henry the Fourth, Part 2,* Samuel B. Hemingway, ed., *The Yale Shakespeare,* act 5, scene 2, lines 122, 129–33.

"Much have I travell'd in the realms of gold . . ." John Keats, "On First Looking Into Chapman's Homer," *College Book of Verse,* pp. 376–77.

"Who hears me, who understands me, becomes mine, a possession for all time . . ." Ralph Waldo Emerson, "Friendship," *Emerson's Essays,* p. 145

"My salad days/When I was green in judgment . . ." Shakespeare, *Antony and Cleopatra,* act 1, scene 5, lines 75–77.

"We, ignorant or ourselves/Beg often our own harms . . ." Shakespeare, *Antony and Cleopatra,* act 2, scene 1, lines 6–9.

"And my spirit, that now so long a time had passed, since trembling in her presence . . ." Dante Alighieri, *Purgatorio,* the Carlyle-Okey-Wickstead translation (New York: Vintage, 1950), canto 30.

"There comes an end to passion . . ." Mary Mercer, work in progress.

"What is heavy? so asketh the load-bearing spirit . . ." Friedrich Nietzsche, *Thus Spake Zarathustra*, Thomas Common, trans. (Modern Library, 1927), p. 23.

"Antagonists as a race . . . become extinct . . ." Johann Wolfgang von Goethe, *Conversations With Eckerman*, John Oxenford, trans. (London: George Bell & Sons, 1883), April 14, 1824.

"It is a great folly to hope that other men will harmonize with us . . ." Goethe, *Conversations With Eckerman*, May 2, 1824.


## Chapter 5

"I know not of aught in the world that so profits a man as taking good counsel with himself . . ." Herodotus, *History of the Greek and Persian War*, George Rawlinson, trans. (New York: Washington Square Press, 1963), p. 255.

"Perverse love must consist in taking a delight in evils that befall others. . . ." Dante, *Purgatorio*, p. 190.

"But in the loneliest wilderness happeneth the second metamorphosis. . . ." Nietzsche, *Thus Spake Zarathustra*, p. 24.

"At last, I have arrived in the First City of the world. . . ." Johann Wolfgang von Goethe, *Goethe: Italian Journey*, W. H. Auden and E. Mayer, trans. (San Francisco, California: North Point Press, 1962), November 1, 1786.

"Every day I cast off a new skin. . . ." Goethe, *Italienische Reise* (München: C. H. Beck, 1978), p. 618. MRJ, trans.

"I shall not say how the scales are falling from my eyes. . . ." Goethe, *Riefe an Charlotte von Stein III* (Leipzig: Insel Verlag, 1907), p. 149. MRJ, trans.

"One must allow a transformation of oneself to occur. . . ." Goethe, *Briefe II* (Hamburg: Christian Wegner Verlag, 1968), p. 43. MRJ, trans.

"From the Duke I received a letter. . . ." Goethe, *Briefe II,* p. 45. MRJ, trans.

"Do not let [anything] come between me and the sun of sublime art and simple humanity. . . ." Goethe, *Italian Journey*, January 6, 1787.

"My existence has now acquired ballast. . . ." Goethe, *Briefe II,* p. 47. MRJ, trans.

"Rome is the only place in the world for an artist, and truly I am nothing other. . . ." Goethe, *Briefe II,* p. 59. MRJ, trans.

"Nature gives everything richly and freely. . . ." Johann Wolfgang von Goethe, "Allerdings: Dem Physiker," *Dictungen, Vol. II* (Leipzig: Insel Verlag, no date), p. 224. MRJ, trans.

"The daughter's daily request for freedom was answered by the daily promise of college. . . ." Mary Mercer, *The Blow upon the Heart*, work in progress.

"Yet must Antony/No way excuse his foils. . . ." Shakespeare, *Antony and Cleopatra*, act 1, scene 4, lines 22–33.

"I long ago lost a hound. . . ." Thoreau, *Walden*, p. 20.

"Direct my mind to God in gratitude, who hath united us with the first star. . . ." Dante Alighieri, *Paradiso*, the Carlyle-Wickstead translation (New York: Vintage, 1959), canto 2.

## *Chapter 6*

"*Lear.* Why came not the slave back to me when I called him? . . ." William Shakespeare, *King Lear*, *The Yale Shakespeare,* act 1, scene 4, lines 53–72, 152–54.

# The Art of Becoming Human

"Dost thou call me a fool, boy? . . . ." Shakespeare, *King Lear*, act 1, scene 4.

"But tell me my brethren, why hath the preying lion still to become a child? . . . ." Friedrich Nietzsche, *Thus Spake Zarathustra*, p. 25.

"When Collatine unwisely did not let/To praise the clear unmatched red and white. . . . ." Shakespeare, *The Rape of Lucrece*, Albert Feuillerat, ed., *The Yale Shakespeare,* lines 10–35.

"*Antonio.* You prove me right yourself in spurning you! . . . ." Johann Wolfgang von Goethe, *Torquato Tasso*, Charles E. Passage, trans. (New York: Friedrich Ungar Publishing, 1977), act 2, lines 1362–1417.

"*Enobarbus.* I have done ill/Of which I do accuse myself so sorely. . . . ." Shakespeare, *Antony and Cleopatra*, act 4, scenes 5 and 7, lines 36–58, 16–17, 19–23.

"The highest to which man can attain is the consciousness of his own ideas and thoughts. . . . ." Johann Wolfgang von Goethe, "Shakespeare und kein Ende," *Aufsätze I* (Leipzig: Insel Verlag, no date), pp. 486–87. MRJ, trans.

"Pierre was hardly changed in his external habits. . . . ." Leo Tolstoy, *War and Peace*, Constance Garnett, trans. (New York: Modern Library, no date), pp. 1030–32.

"Her eyes are fled/Into the deep dark cabins of her head. . . . ." William Shakespeare, "Venus and Adonis," *Shakespeare's Poems*, Albert Feuillerat, ed., *The Yale Shakespeare,* p. 38, lines 1037–42.

"O Light eternal, who only in thyself abidest. . . . ." Dante, *Paradiso*, canto 33.